SO-FBW-153

Contents

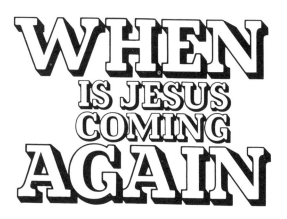

WHEN IS JESUS COMING AGAIN

by Hal Lindsey and others

Creation House
Carol Stream, Illinois

ISBN 0-88419-110-9
Library of Congress Catalog Card Number 75-3613

ABOUT THE AUTHORS

Gleason L. Archer   Robert H. Gundry   Hal Lindsey

Gleason L. Archer, Jr., professor and chairman of the division of Old Testament at Trinity Divinity School, received his A.M. and Ph.D. from Harvard Graduate School; his LL.B. from Suffolk U. Law School. Listed in the 1971 edition of Outstanding Educators of America, Archer has authored several books including In the Shadow of the Cross (a translation of Jerome's Commentary on Daniel) and Survey of Old Testament Introduction.

Robert H. Gundry, 41, is chairman of the department of religious studies, Westmont College. He received his B.A. and B.D. from Los Angeles Baptist College and Seminary; his Ph.D. from The University, Manchester, England, with lengthy periods of study at the U. of Basel, Switzerland, and the U. of Edinburgh, Scotland. His book, A Survey of the New Testament, was published by Zondervan, as was The Church and the Tribulation (1973). The Gundrys have three children.

Hal Lindsey presently teaches in a three-year Biblical training school called The Light and Power House, located near the UCLA campus in Westwood, California. One of the first contemporary writers to make Biblical prophecy an accepted and stimulating subject in the secular world at large, Lindsey is author of several bestselling books, including The Late Great Planet Earth and There's a New World Coming.

Thomas S. McCall, 37, received his B.A. from the U. of Texas; his B.D. and Th.M. from Talbot Theo. Sem.; his Th.D. from Dallas Theo. Sem. He has co-authored (with Zola Levitt) two books: Satan in the Sanctuary and The Coming Russian Invasion of Israel (Moody). McCall is missionary-in-charge, Southwestern District, American Board of Missions to the Jews.

Arnold T. Olson is president of the Evangelical Free Church of America and past president of the National Association of Evangelicals. He is administratively active in the American Bible Society and the United Bible Societies and is on the board of directors for the American Institute of Holy Land Studies in Jerusalem. A contributing editor to The Evangelical Beacon, Olson has published several books, including This We Believe and Inside Jerusalem—City of Destiny.

J. Barton Payne, 51, received his B.D. from San Francisco Theo. Sem.; his Th.M. and Ph.D. from Princeton Theo. Sem. Currently he is professor of Old Testament at Covenant Theo. Sem., St. Louis. The Paynes attend the Reformed Presbyterian Church, Evangelical Synod; have four sons and a daughter.

Thomas S. McCall   Arnold T. Olson   J. Barton Payne

FOREWORD

One of the most perplexing questions of our day is, "When will Jesus come again?"

Pretribulationists have one theory; midtribulationists another; posttribulationists still another. And did you know that there are pasttribulationists who say that the pre-, mid- and posttribulationists are wrong?

Here is an overview—one of the first and most easily understood—of each of the major positions on what the Bible calls the Great Tribulation (Matthew 24:21), "For then there will be a great tribulation, such as has not occurred since the beginning of the world until now, nor ever shall."

Written for laymen by leading exponents of each view, this compilation presents the total picture of the end times.

When you're through, you'll either know why you've always believed as you have—or you will discover you prefer another viewpoint. In either case, you'll be more eager to share with others the "blessed hope" of the coming again of Jesus.

One caution. Pray as you read. And re-member that an equally devout Christian has presented each view—even if you do not agree with it.

Prophets predicted the Second Coming of Jesus Christ. Here is a convincing summation of their prophecies—along with a fine collection of Jesus' own promises of His return.

INTRODUCTION

THE SECOND COMING A CERTAINTY

BY ARNOLD T. OLSON

> Ye men of Galilee, why stand ye gazing up into heaven? This same Jesus, which is taken up from you into heaven, shall so come in like manner as ye have seen him go into heaven (Acts 1:11).

Ever since the first days of the Christian church, evangelical Christians have been "looking for that blessed hope, and the glorious appearing of the great God and our Savior Jesus Christ," They may have disagreed as to its timing and to the events on the eschatological calendar. They may have differed as to a pretribulation or posttribulation rapture— the the pre- or post- or non-millennial coming. They may have been divided as to a literal rebirth of Israel. However, all are agreed that the final solution to the problems of this world is in the hands of the King of kings who will someday make the kingdoms of this world His very own.

At times in history the flame of hope has burned brightly in the darkness of persecu-

9

tion. At other times the entire church has been asleep, but waiting nonetheless. For all that, as Bible believers we are united in looking for a personal return of our Lord and Savior Jesus Christ.

The evidence in the Word of God as to the certainty and the importance of that event is overwhelming. In fact, the first prophetic utterance by man deals with Christ's second, not His first, coming. Jude says in verse 14 of his epistle that "Enoch also, the seventh from Adam, prophesied of these, saying, Behold, the Lord cometh with ten thousand of his saints." This prediction is also the final word from Jesus as He promises, "Surely I come quickly" (Revelation 22:20).

Between these two utterances more is written about the return of Jesus than about any other doctrine. More than fifteen hundred passages in the Old Testament and three hundred in the New contain promises of His return. These do not include the many additional passages that deal with matters relating to this event.

In discussing the return of Jesus we will not enter into such details as His coming for or with His saints or the establishment of an earthly or heavenly kingdom. We will not even seek to differentiate between the possible phases of that return. We are limiting ourselves to the following:

1. The prophets predicted the second coming of Christ.
2. Jesus promised it.
3. The apostles preached it.
4. The church pronounced it.
5. Reason predicates it.
6. Heaven's ambassadors pinpoint it.

THE PROPHETS PREDICTED THE SECOND COMING OF CHRIST

The same men of God who were moved by the Spirit to predict in accurate detail the first coming of Jesus had even more to say about His return. Since they proved themselves so accurate in the former case, is it not reasonable to accept their statements as to the latter?

Moses gives the test of a prophet in Deuteronomy 18:22: "When a prophet speaketh in the name of the Lord, if the thing follow not, nor come to pass, that is the thing which the Lord hath not spoken, but the prophet hath spoken it presumptuously: thou shalt not be afraid of him."

Consider some of the predictions about His first coming and then a few regarding His return. Moses in the above passage predicts the coming of the Prophet (Deuteronomy 18:15-22). People in the time of Christ recognized Him as a literal fulfillment of that prediction: "Philip findeth Nathanael, and saith unto him, We have found him, of whom

Moses in the law, and the prophets did write, Jesus of Nazareth, the son of Joseph" (John 1:45). Peter calls attention to it in his sermon in the temple: "For Moses truly said unto the fathers, A prophet shall the Lord your God raise up unto you of your brethren" (Acts 3:22).

Many Old Testament predictions concerning details of Jesus' first coming are carefully identified in their fulfillment:

He was to be born of a virgin (Isaiah 7:14; Matthew 1:22-23).

He was to be of the family of David (Isaiah 11:1; Luke 1:32).

Little children would be massacred (Jeremiah 31:15; Matthew 2:16-18).

Jesus as a child would be taken to Egypt and later returned (Hosea 11:1; Matthew 2:15).

He would grow up in Galilee (Isaiah 9:1; Matthew 2:22-23).

He would be anointed by the Holy Spirit (Isaiah 11:2; Luke 4:17-21).

He would enter Jerusalem on a donkey (Zechariah 9:9; Matthew 21:4-5).

He would be betrayed by one of His followers (Psalm 41:9; John 13:18).

His disciples would desert Him in His hour of need (Zechariah 13:7; Matthew 26:31).

He would be sold for thirty pieces of silver which would eventually be used to purchase a potter's field (Zechariah 11:12-13; Matthew 26:15; 27:7, 10).

He would be the object of spitting and buffeting (Isaiah 50:6; Matthew 27:30).

He would be offered gall and vinegar (Psalm 69:21; Matthew 27:34, 48).

In His crucifixion, not one bone would be broken (Exodus 12:46; John 19:33, 36).

His garments would be divided by lot (Psalm 22:18; John 19:23-24).

He would be put to death amid criminals but buried with the rich (Isaiah 53:9; Matthew 27:38, 57-60).

Certainly this is enough evidence to give credence to the prediction about a literal second coming which is first recorded by Moses in Deuteronomy 30:3: "That then the Lord thy God will turn thy captivity, and have compassion upon thee, and *will return* and gather thee from all the nations, whither the Lord thy God hath scattered thee." It continues through the law, the Psalms, and the prophets. We quote but two of the more than fifteen hundred passages since they are most literally related to our text:

> Behold, the day of the Lord cometh, and thy spoil shall be divided in the midst of thee. For I will gather all nations against Jerusalem to battle; and the city shall be taken, and the houses rifled, and the women ravished; and half of the city shall go forth into captivity, and the residue of the people shall not be cut off from the city. Then shall the Lord go forth, and fight against those nations, as when he fought in the day of battle. And his feet shall stand in that day upon

the mount of Olives, which is before Jerusalem on the east, and the mount of Olives shall cleave in the midst thereof toward the east and toward the west, and there shall be a very great valley; and half of the mountain shall remove toward the north, and half of it toward the south (Zechariah 14:1-4).

And I will pour upon the house of David, and upon the inhabitants of Jerusalem, the spirit of grace and of supplications: and they shall look upon me whom they have pierced, and they shall mourn for him, as one mourneth for his only son and shall be in bitterness for him, as one that is in bitterness for his firstborn" (Zechariah 12:10).

Other pertinent passages include Psalm 2:1-9, 24:1-10, 50:1-5, 96:10-13, 110:1; Isaiah 9:7, 11:10-12, 63:1-6; Jeremiah 23:5-6; Ezekiel 37:21-22; Daniel 2:44-45, 7:13-14; Hosea 3:4-5; Micah 4:7; Zechariah 2:10-12, 6:12-13, 13:6.

JESUS PROMISED HE WOULD RETURN

Jesus predicted events which occurred in His own lifetime and some that would take place later. He passes the test of a true prophet. Why should we doubt His promises to come again?

He predicted His betrayal (Matthew 26:21; John 6:64).

He predicted His denial (Matthew 26:34).

He predicted a scattering of His followers (John 16:32).

He predicted His crucifixion (Matthew 26:2).

He promised His resurrection (John 2:19-22)

He promised the Holy Spirit (John 16:7-15)

He revealed plans to build His church (Matthew 16:18).

He predicted the destruction of the temple (Mark 13:2).

He predicted the destruction of Jerusalem (Luke 19:41-44).

He predicted the end of Gentile domination of the city (Luke 21:24).

He promised to come again (John 14:1-3).

Some of these pronouncements are comforting, others disturbing. Some were expressly given as promises, others in the form of parables or in our Lord's eschatologica discourses.

Let not your heart be troubled: ye believe in God, believe also in me. In my Father's house are many mansions: if it were not so, I would have told you. I go to prepare a place for you. And if I go and prepare a place for you, I will come again, and receive you unto myself; that where I am, there ye may be also (John 14:1-3).

Ye have heard how I said unto you, I go away, and come again unto you (John. 14:28a).

Jesus saith unto him, If I will that he tarry till I come, what is that to thee? Follow thou me [John 21:22].

Be ye therefore ready also: for the Son of man cometh at an hour when ye think not [Luke 12:40].

I tell you that he will avenge them speedily. Nevertheless when the Son of man cometh, shall he find faith on the earth? [Luke 18:8].

For as the lightning cometh out of the east, and shineth even unto the west; so shall also the coming of the Son of man be [Matthew 24:27].

Watch therefore: for ye know not what hour your Lord doth come [Matthew 24:42].

When the Son of man shall come in his glory, and all the holy angels with him, then shall he sit upon the throne of his glory [Matthew 25:31].

THE APOSTLES PREACHED THE SECOND COMING OF CHRIST

The apostles got the message! There was no doubt in their minds that Christ's return was certain. They preached the Jesus who died, who rose again, and who was coming again. The passages are too numerous to quote fully.

For as in Adam all die, even so in Christ shall all be made alive. But every man in his own order: Christ the firstfruits; afterward they that are Christ's at his coming [1 Corinthians 15:22-23].

For they themselves shew of us what manner of entering in we had unto you, and how ye turned to God from idols to serve the living and true God; and to wait for his Son from heaven, whom he raised from the dead, even Jesus, which delivered us from the wrath to come [1 Thessalonians 1:9-10].

For the Lord himself shall descend from heaven with a shout (1 Thessalonians 4:16).

. . . and not to me only, but unto all them also that love his appearing (2 Timothy 4:8).

So Christ was once offered to bear the sins of many; and unto them that look for him shall he appear the second time without sin unto salvation [Hebrews 9:28].

Wherefore gird up the loins of your mind, be sober, and hope to the end for the grace that is to be brought unto you at the revelation of Jesus Christ [1 Peter 1:13].

THE CHURCH HAS PRONOUNCED THE SECOND COMING OF CHRIST

The first Christians believed that Christ was coming again. In fact, so certain were they of His return that they expected it in their lifetime. Those dying were presumed to have missed the great event. Christ's return was part of the original belief of the church and it was reiterated by the church Fathers and the creeds through the ensuing centuries.

The church Fathers believed in the second coming. Ignatius of Antioch (35-107?) wrote: "Christ was received up to the Father and sits on his right hand, waiting til his enemies are put under his feet." Irenaeus (130-202?) said, "Appearing from heaven in the Glory of the Father, to comprehend all things under one head." Tertullian (160-220?) said, "He will come again with glory."

The creeds of the church confess His coming. Millions of believers throughout the centuries have repeated the words in the Apostles' Creed, "from whence he shall come to judge the quick and the dead."

Other confessions have witnessed to it.

The Augsburg Confession (1530): "Also they [the churches] teach that, in the consummation of the world [at the last day], Christ shall appear to judge, and shall raise up all the dead, and shall give unto the godly and elect eternal life and everlasting joy; but ungodly men and the devils shall he condemn into endless torments."

The Belgic Confession (1561): "Our Lord Jesus Christ will come from heaven, corporally and visibly, as he ascended with great glory and majesty."

The Heidelberg Catechism (1563): "In all my sorrows and persecutions, with uplifted head, I look for the selfsame One who has before offered himself for me."

The Thirty-nine Articles of the Church of England (1571): "He ascended into Heaven, and there sitteth, until he return."

The Westminster Confession (1647): "As Christ would have us to be certainly persuaded that there shall be a day of judgment, both to deter all men from sin, and for the greater consolation of the godly in their adversity: so he will have that day unknown to men, that they may shake off carnal security, and be always watchful, because they know not at what hour the Lord will come; and may be ever prepared to say, Come, Lord Jesus, come quickly. Amen."

The confession of the Congregational Union of England and Wales (1833): "They believe that Christ will finally come to judge the whole human race according to their works."

The New Hampshire Baptist Confession,

one of the earlier Baptist statements (1833): "We believe that the end of the world is approaching, that at the last day Christ will descend from heaven, and raise the dead from the grave to final retribution; that a solemn separation will then take place."

The first-known formal confession of my own church, the Confession of the Evangelical Free Church of Geneva (1848): "We expect from heaven our Savior Jesus Christ, who will change our body of humiliation and make it conform to his own body of glory; and we believe that, in that day, the dead who are in Christ, coming out from their tombs at his voice, and the faithful then living on the earth, all transformed through his power, will be taken up together into the clouds to meet him, and thus we shall always be with the Savior."

Most of the statements were somber in nature. Even though the spirit of a "blessed hope" seems to be missing, the fact of Christ's second coming was surely believed. Could so many church bodies, seeking to base their doctrinal statements on the Bible, be correct in pronouncements on the authority of Scripture, the deity of Christ, and the effectiveness of His atonement, and have been so wrong for two thousand years in declaring our Lord's return?

The pronouncements were not just made in the distant past. Even such a controversial document as the Presbyterian Confession of 1967 states: "The life, death and resurrection and promised coming of Jesus Christ have set the pattern for Church mission."

Two of the most evangelically ecumenical and representative meetings in recent history reaffirm belief in His return. The Congress on the Church's Worldwide Mission (1966), in what is now known as the Wheaton Declaration, states: "The Scriptures emphatically declare that Christ will return when the gathering out of His true Church is completed. All human history shall be consummated in Him. We must affirm this confidence."

The World Congress on Evangelism in Berlin in 1966 declared the same: "Evangelism is the proclamation of the Gospel of the crucified and risen Christ, the only Redeemer of men, according to the Scriptures, with the purpose of persuading condemned and lost sinners to put their trust in God by receiving and accepting Christ as Savior through the power of the Holy Spirit, and to serve Christ as Lord in every calling of life and in the fellowship of His Church, looking toward the day of His coming."

No, this is not just some ancient view long since outgrown. A Gallup Poll reported that over three and one half times as many Americans as voted for Richard M. Nixon in the 1968 election believe in the second coming of Christ.

Nor is it only a matter of church pronouncements, resolutions, formulas and creeds. Over and beyond all this, it is a feeling as well as a faith—a fervent hope as well as a doctrinal statement. Many have felt what Martin Luther articulated, "I live as though Jesus Christ died yesterday, rose again today and were coming again tomorrow."

The late church historian Kenneth Scott Latourette confessed, "I believe that our Lord may return at any time and bring this present stage of history to an end. That may well come between now and the year 2000."

How moving the moment when the Archbishop of Canterbury quoted from the coronation ceremony as he handed the crown to Queen Elizabeth II: "I give thee, O Sovereign Lady, this crown to wear, until He who reserves the right to wear it shall return."

Or the native leader in the jungle of the Congo, so recently out of primitive paganism, who said in his welcoming remarks to me, "We have waited a long time for the chief to come and inspect our work." Naming mission executives and other church leaders who had visited the field, he added after each name, "But he was not the chief." Then he concluded, "Now the chief is come and there is only one thing left to wait for, and that is the coming of our Lord from heaven."

THE AMBASSADOR FROM HEAVEN HAS
PINPOINTED THE SECOND COMING

Christ's return is to be personal. There are
those who say that Christ has already
returned—that He came back on the day of
Pentecost or that He returned through the
Christian church. Others see His return in the
tractor on the farm, the washing machine in
the home, the eight-hour day, decrees forcing
desegregation, the antipoverty programs, the
peace movements, literacy for the masses,
medical care for all people. But heaven says it
is Jesus Himself who shall return.

Christ is to be recognizable. It is the same
Jesus—the one who walked, who taught, who
healed, who mended broken hearts, who
showed us the Father, who was raised from the
dead in this very city of Jerusalem—who will
return. It is significant that the name Jesus is
used—not the Christ, the Son of the living God,
true though that is. In this context it is
Jesus—this same Jesus—free from all the
theological formulas, the misrepresentations,
the philosophical interpretations.

In the light of this fact, a current situation is
of special significance to me personally: The
growing interest by Jewish scholars in Israel
in Jesus of Nazareth. David Ben-Gurion said in
1961, "Christianity stemmed from the Jewish
people, its inspiration was from a Jew whose
ideas belonged within the framework of

Jewish concepts in his day." On one of my recent visits, a government press officer referred to a certain scholar and said, "That man walks Jesus, thinks Jesus, loves Jesus but he still is an Orthodox Jew." Another scholar told me how he disliked the name, the Church of the Holy Sepulchre. "It should be," he said, "the Church of the Resurrection, for the event is far more important than the place."

I was told during a visit in 1967 that in the four previous years, twenty-three books had been written by Jews about Jesus. I asked if they were derogatory. My informant replied most emphatically, "No, but the writers are Jews, some of them Orthodox Jews." It shows a new interest in Jesus and a desire to rediscover Him. This informant also indicated that one of the fastest-growing departments at the Hebrew University is the Department of Christian Studies, whose students are atheists, agnostics, evangelical Christians, Catholic priests and Orthodox Jews.

Dr. Saul Colby of the Religious Affairs Department notes, "Lectures on the New Testament by Jews, who, out of penetrating familiarity with Hebrew sources, are equipped to present, illuminatingly, the historical and spiritual background of early Christianity, attract many listeners." Professor David Flusser has often expressed the view that Jesus belongs in the rabbinical tradition. One of the Orthodox Jews said years ago, "Oh, that we could only know who this Jesus is, and what is His true relation to us wanderers." A rabbi confided, "I believe Jesus lives: I find it possible to believe He performed miracles; I even believe He could have risen from the dead; but I do not believe He was the Son of God." I am convinced that there are a number of Israelis who know Jesus the man better than many Christians do. It is this same Jesus, the object of so much research, who will return.

The second coming is to be visible. "[He] shall so come in like manner as ye have seen him go into heaven" (Acts 1:11). "They shall see the Son of man coming in the clouds of heaven" (Matthew 24:30). "Then shall they see the Son of man" (Mark 13:26). "And every eye shall see him" (Revelation 1:7).

When before in human history could everyone have been an eyewitness to His coming? Today, satellites and video tapes along with television can provide every person with a view of His coming.

The place will be locatable. He is to come back in the same manner as He ascended, and to the same place: "His feet shall stand in that day upon the mount of Olives, which is before Jerusalem on the east (Zechariah 14:4).

CONCLUSION

The angels not only pinpointed our Lord's return but also asked a pertinent question:

"Why stand ye gazing up into heaven?" This brought the disciples back to reality and they obeyed the final command of Jesus to first tarry for power and then to get going—not to gaze but to go.

We are not assembled here to gaze but to be reminded anew of the imminency of our Lord's return and the pressing need to let the whole world know that the Bridegroom cometh. Opinions may differ on the details of His coming, but we stand united in our belief that He will indeed return—He will return soon—He must, in fact, return soon.

We are here to claim once again one of the last promises of the Old Testament, namely, "But unto you that fear my name shall the Sun of righteousness arise with healing in his wings" (Malachi 4:2), and to join with all the saints of all the ages in the final prayer of the New Testament: "Even so, come, Lord Jesus" (Revelation 22:20). We are not gazing, not speculating, not arguing, but waiting for our Savior, and while we wait, we work.

Several years ago, when I returned from my first trip to the Orient, my wife came to the Minneapolis airport to meet me. She was surprised to find our pastor and a few other men from the local congregation in front of the flight information board. "We've come," they said, "to see how you two greet one another when your husband returns from one of his journeys." Then they turned back to the board and asked, "Is he on Western's flight from Los Angeles or San Francisco? Is he coming, perhaps, on a Northwest flight from Seattle or Portland? What is the flight number? Is the plane on time? What is the gate number?" My wife, of course, knew the details, for she had been in touch with me. So she proceeded directly to the arrival gate. When we returned to the main part of the terminal, the men were still in discussion. God forbid that we should be so busy gazing or simply discussing Christ's coming that He will not find us waiting for Him. Whether we hope to meet Him in the air or at the Mount of Olives, we know He will arrive on time. Beyond everything else, may we be ready to meet this same Jesus.

We wait for a great and glorious day,
As many as love the Lord,
When shadows shall flee, and clouds pass away,
And weeping no more be heard.

In glory and pow'r our King shall appear,
And call to Himself His own;
No distance, nor death shall part them as here,
Nor sin, with its pains, be known.

For crosses we've borne then crowns will be
    giv'n,
For tempests, eternal calm;
For pathway of thorns, rich mansions in heav'n,
For warfare, the victor's palm.

We know not the day, we know not the hour,
When sounds the last trump so clear;
But loud rings a cry from truth's lofty tow'r.
"The day of the Lord is near."

O Wonderful day that soon may be here!
O beautiful hope the pilgrim to cheer!
Thy coming we hail in tuneful accord,
Thou glorious day of Christ, our Lord.

A.L. Skoog

Twenty pieces of an "end times" pattern are unmistakably coming together simultaneously for the first time in history.

CHAPTER 1

PREDICTION OF FUTURE EVENTS

BY HAL LINDSEY

As the world reels under the impact of the latest Middle East crisis, many are discovering that the events are fitting into a larger pattern of precisely-predicted events.

The pattern is to be found woven through the Hebrew prophets from Moses to Jesus Christ and John the Apostle. The prophecies were made during a period of from 3500 to 1900 years ago.

Throughout these predictions, it's clear that the events are to lead to a final seven-year period of world catastrophe. This period will climax with a global war of such magnitude that only the personal, visible return of Jesus Christ to this planet will prevent man from self-annihilation.

THINGS WE ARE SEEING

Listed below are 20 pieces of this pattern which are unmistakably coming together simultaneously for the first time in history:

* The return of the dispersed Jews to Israel to become a nation again in 1948.
* The Jews' recapture of the Old City of Jerusalem in the 1967 Arab-Israeli War.
* The rise of Russia as a powerful nation and enemy of Israel.
* The Arab confederation against the new State of Israel.
* The rise of a military power in the Orient that can field an army of 200 million soldiers. (Red China alone boasts that she has this number of troops!)
* The revival of the Old Roman Empire in the form of a ten-nation confederacy. (I believe the European Common Market is ultimately going to be this power.)
* The revival of the dark occultic practices of ancient Babylon.
* The unprecedented turn to drugs.
* The increase of international revolution.
* The increase of wars.
* The increase of earthquakes.
* The increase of famines through the population explosion.
* The coming of plagues.
* The increase of pollution.
* The departure of many Christian churches from the historic truth of Christianity.
* The move toward a one-world religion.
* The move toward a one-world government.
* The decline of the United States as a major world power.

* The increase in lawlessness.
* The decline of the family unit.

The Arabs will continue to bring greater pressure upon the Western nations to support their demands against Israel. They will do so through the continued restriction of oil without which the industrial nations cannot survive. They may begin to use their vast financial power to seriously threaten the economy of the United States as well. It is doubtful that Fort Knox could back up the dollars they hold, if they demanded gold for them.

The United States will have some severe economic shocks from the European Common Market and the Arab oil squeeze. It will continue its decline as a major power both by this and internal moral decadence.

The European Common Market will begin to emerge as the greatest economic power in history.

Israel will continue to increasingly become the Western world's dilemma. The Middle East will continue to be the most dangerous threat to world peace in history. The prophets clearly say that the spark that sets off Armageddon will be struck by the invasion of Israel by the Egyptian-led Arabs and the Russians.

Jesus predicted these days we're living in

when He said concerning the prophetic signs, "When you see all these things, know He is at the door ready to return." Then He said, "This generation will not pass away until all is fulfilled."

My opinion is that, because we are seeing all these signs fitting into the predicted pattern, we are the generation which will see the culmination of history, as we know it, and the return of Christ. Who knows, perhaps this will be the year of Christ's sudden and mysterious coming to snatch out all those who believe in Him.

Born-again believers will be taken to glory before the Lord allows the terrible events of the tribulation to convulse the earth.

CHAPTER 2

JESUS IS COMING AGAIN: PRETRIBULATION

BY THOMAS S. McCALL

The young man had no idea this was to be the day of the rapture. He stepped out of his house, eased into his car, and headed off to work as he had a thousand mornings before. He pulled up to a stop sign, halted the car, and sat there dully, watching the traffic pass by.

Suddenly he heard an overwhelming noise above, an ear-piercing cry out of the skies. An instant later he was conscious of a rousing trumpet-like blast. The sounds reached him in rapid, mind-numbing succession, and he reeled from the shock.

To his astonishment he rose through the roof of the car, and felt his body change through a complete metamorphosis! Like a butterfly escaping its cocoon, his flesh shed its mortality, and took on immortality. Miraculous eternal life infused his exhilarated being as he soared upward into the clouds.

Gradually his eyes focused and became

transfixed on the magnificent presence of his Lord drawing him upward like a magnet to Himself. He managed to look around as he flashed through the air and realized an enormous multitude of people were racing along with him toward a great rendezvous in the air, to meet the Lord Jesus Christ. They had become "like Him," seeing Him face to face. When the whole crowd arrived at the Lord's side, He gathered them together, and they all went home with Him!

Down below, on the earth, a long line of irritated drivers honked furiously at the deserted car at the stop sign.

It had a sticker on the rear bumper: "Warning—In Case of Rapture, This Car Will Be Unmanned!"

This prophetic scenario is the cherished hope of millions of believers in Christ. They yearn for the imminent moment when the Lord will come to take them suddenly to Himself in the event called the rapture.[1] They are convinced that this transforming experience will climax the church age and that all born-again believers will be taken to heaven before the Lord allows the terrible events of the tribulation to convulse the earth. So these Christians believe in what is called the *pretribulation rapture.*

---

1. The term "Rapture" is derived from *rapere*, the Latin translation of "caught up" in the Vulgate, I Thessalonians 4:17.

Whether or not the Church[2] will have to go through the tribulation is no light matter. If we have to endure the tyranny of the Antichrist, the wrathful judgment of God on the earth, the abomination of desolation in the future Temple,[3] the devastation of the Armageddon war, and the horrendous destruction of vegetation, water and life that will occur during the tribulation, we had better know about it and prepare for it the best we can. On the other hand, if we are to look for the imminent appearance of Christ in the air before the tribulation, to take us to be forever with Him, we should be awake and alive to that glorious prospect.

So what are the vital issues before us? What are the specific views about the rapture and its relationship to believers? Before going any further, let's define our terms:

Pretribulation rapture—all true believers in Christ will be caught up in the air to go with the Lord to heaven suddenly, at any moment, before the tribulation begins. The rapture will include all believers throughout the church age, whether living or dead, at which time they will receive their eternal heavenly bodies, like Christ's resurrection body. Following

2. Our use of the term "Church" in this chapter refers to genuine born-again believers in Christ. It does not refer to those professing Christians who have not personally received Christ. Those unbelievers will continue on the earth into the tribulation and will be part of the universal false religion of the time.

3. See *Satan in the Sanctuary*, Thomas S. McCall and Zola Levitt (Moody Press, 1973), for the complete story of the Jerusalem Temple—past, present and future.

the rapture is the tribulation, the return of Christ to the earth, the millennium and the eternal new heaven and new earth.

Postribulation rapture—believers will continue on the earth through the tribulation period. At the end of the tribulation, believers will be caught up to be with the Lord and immediately return to earth with Him for the millennium.

Midtribulation rapture—believers will remain on the earth for the first 3½ years of the 7-year tribulation, and will be caught up before the last 3½ years (the great tribulation) falls upon the human race.

Partial rapture—only spiritual believers in Christ will be caught up before the tribulation. Carnal believers will have to suffer through the wrath of the tribulation along with the rest of the world.

No rapture—there is no rapture, no tribulation period, no millennium. Believers look forward only to the eternal state of heaven in the future.

Which teaching is true? Which view of the rapture does the Bible teach? I believe that the pretribulation rapture view is correct, and that it reflects in proper perspective all that the Bible teaches on the rapture and the tribulation.

It is beyond the scope of this chapter to marshall all of the arguments for and against the pretribulation rapture view. This has been done well in several scholarly works[4]. What I hope to do here is to whet your spiritual appetite to conduct a personal study of the Scriptures for yourself about the great truth of the imminent rapture.

The Bible teaches that the rapture will occur when all believers of the church age, living and dead, are taken up to heaven to be with the Lord: "For the Lord himself shall descend from heaven with a shout, with the voice of the archangel, and with the trump of God; and the dead in Christ shall rise first. Then we which are alive and remain shall be caught up together with them in the clouds, to meet the Lord in the air; and so shall we ever be with the Lord" (I Thessalonians 4:16-17 KJV. See also John 14:3 and I Corinthians 15:51-53).

But the tribulation is a horse of a different color. Jesus said the tribulation will be so horrible that the world will have never seen anything like it before and never would afterwards: "For then shall be the great tribulation, such as was not since the beginning of the world to this time, no, nor ever shall be" (Matthew 24:21 KJV).

Think of all the upheavals humanity has experienced throughout the centuries: wars, earthquakes, famines, floods, tornadoes, monsoons, and persecutions. But they are minor irritations compared to the tribulation.

4. See John F. Walvoord, *The Rapture Question* (Zondervan 1973); and Gerald Stanton, *Kept from the Hour* (Zondervan 1956).

Christ declares that none of these previous calamities holds a candle to the horrors of the tribulation. Such terrible wars, such devastation of earth's natural resources, such destruction of human life, are unimaginable to us who live in relative tranquility.

At least one billion people will be exterminated during the tribulation! We learn this from Revelation 9:15 which declares that at the designated time, supernatural power will be turned loose "to slay the third part of men." The bulging population of the earth is today estimated at something over four billion people. But experts on the population explosion indicate that the number could be six billion in a few years, making the tribulation casualty rate jump to a possible two billion deaths!

We cannot conceive of the full effect of the sudden loss of one third of mankind. Many horrible events will occur during the tribulation, but this statistic alone should be sufficient to alert us to the extreme devastation which will take place during the time of God's wrath.

Which event, then, do we expect first? Is it the "blessed hope" of the rapture, or the "wrath" of the tribulation which we are to anticipate? It has to be one or the other. Either we are looking for the rapture to remove us or we are looking for the tribulation to consume us.

I believe the rapture will come first.

Many evidences in the Bible prove that the rapture must come before the tribulation.[5] I will enumerate some of them.

First, the rapture belongs to the Church, while the tribulation belongs to Israel and the nations. It is complete confusion to have the Church of born-again believers going through the tribulation. In reality, the tribulation is equivalent to the seventieth week of Daniel, and concerns the people of Israel, not the Church. The Lord's angel told Daniel that the prophecy of the "weeks" had to do with "thy people (Israel) and thy holy city (Jerusalem)" (Daniel 9:24). The New Testament Church, composed of believing Jews and Gentiles in this age, is nowhere in sight. The Church must therefore be removed out of the earth via the rapture before God's tribulation dealings with Israel and the "time of Jacob's trouble" can be started.

Second, the restraining Holy Spirit must be removed before the Antichrist is revealed. Paul instructed the Thessalonians that "he who now letteth (hindereth) will let until he be taken out of the way. And then shall the Wicked be revealed" (II Thessalonians 2:6-8). In other words, the Antichrist will not be unveiled until the hinderer is removed. The great inhibitor of evil must be none other than

5. See Walvoord's book, *The Rapture Question,* which lists 50 reasons why the rapture must come before the tribulation.

the Holy Spirit of God. Since the Spirit is particularly associated with and indwells the believing Church, that group of people will have to be removed from the scene when the Spirit is removed. The equation is The Restrainer (= the Holy Spirit = the Indweller and Energizer of believers) must be taken out of the way before the Wicked One is revealed (= the beginning of the tribulation). So the tribulation cannot start until the Church is raptured.

Third, the purpose of the rapture is to deliver the Church, while the purpose of the tribulation is to judge the unbelieving world. The above quoted passage in II Thessalonians 2, goes on to inform us of the Antichrist "whose coming is . . . with all deceivableness of unrighteousness in them that perish . . . that they all might be judged . . . But God hath from the beginning chosen you to salvation" (verses 9-13). No purpose would be served by dragging the Church into the awesome judgment prescribed for the unbelieving world. Just as the Lord brought righteous Lot out of Sodom before judging that city with destruction, so He will extract us out of the world who have trusted in Him before He judges the unbelievers with destruction. The grace of the rapture must precede the wrath of the tribulation.

Fourth, the rapture is imminent and could occur at any moment. No tribulation period signs are required before it occurs. The Bible commands us to be constantly "looking for that blessed hope, and the glorious appearing of the great God and our Savior, Jesus Christ" (Titus 2:13). There are no prerequisite signs for the rapture, and nothing prophetic has to occur before this "blessed hope." But the tribulation is full of signs and portents. There is the covenant between the Antichrist and Israel, the abomination of desolation in the revived Jerusalem Temple, and the war of Armageddon, to mention a few. These are signs in the tribulation to warn the world of coming judgment. To have all of these signs occurring while the Church is still on the earth would make the Scriptural exhortations for the Church to await the imminent return of the Lord in the air meaningless. Since the rapture is imminent, there can be no intervening tribulation signs before it occurs.

Look up. The Lord might return before you finish this chapter!

All of these truths are highly persuasive, and assure us that the rapture will come before the tribulation. If you are not a believer in Christ yet, take this opportunity now—before it's too late—to put your trust in the Lord Jesus who loved you and died for you. Have confidence in the One who arose from the dead, and He will give you an eternal body like His when He comes. You can pray to Him something like this:

"Lord Jesus, I don't want to go through the terrible tribulation or the final judgment of lost people. I believe right now that You died for my sins and are alive today. Please give me Your life—and when You come for Your own at the rapture, I will look forward to flying up to meet You in the air. Thanks."

Maybe you are already a believer in Christ, but have just become aware of the awesome significance of the meaning of the pretribulation rapture. Perhaps you would like to express a heartfelt concern to our Living Christ:

"Lord Jesus, how can I ever thank You enough for forgiving me and giving me Your eternal life and joy? I am awaiting with eager anticipation the rapture when I will be able to see You like You are. It will be great to have the spiritual body You have promised me. The only bad thing about it is that so many friends, relatives and people living here do not know You and will have to go through Your tremendous judgment during the tribulation. Please give me the wisdom and energy to share Your message of redemption with as many as possible, so they can join us when You come for us. I can hardly wait for that wonderful day of the rapture. Please make it soon. Thank you very much."

So how do you feel about this issue now? My hope is that you are rejoicing that, as a believer, you will not have to go through the awesome tribulation, and that you will be able to observe those events with the Lord from a balcony seat in heaven. See you at the rapture!

Even so, come quickly, Lord Jesus.

If the great tribulation begins with the out-pouring of the wrath of God upon the world, then the sudden deliverance of the Church will take place after the first three-and-one-half years of the final seven.

CHAPTER 3

JESUS IS COMING AGAIN: MIDTRIBULATION

BY GLEASON ARCHER

Between the competing views of the pretribulation and the posttribulation rapture stands a mediating option, the theory of the midseventieth-week rapture. Some refer to it as the midtribulation rapture, as though this sudden deliverance of the Church were to take place after the first 3½ years of the final seven before the return of Christ to establish His kingdom on earth. But if the great tribulation is regarded as commencing with the outpouring of the wrath of God upon the world as described in Revelation 16-18, then it is hardly accurate to describe the midweek view as a midtribulation theory, for it is really a form of pretribulation rapturism which limits the time interval of climactic world suffering to the final 3½ years prior to the battle of Armageddon. To me, this approach seems to offer fewer problems than either of the other views, as I will show you.

In the first place, it is significant that

chapters 7, 9 and 12 of Daniel, as well as chapters 11 and 12 of Revelation, attach great importance to 3½ years (or forty-two months) as the time when some great event will mark the midpoint of the final seven years of pre-Kingdom history. It is reasonable to suppose that this event will be nothing less than the fulfillment of I Thessalonians 4:15-17, the sudden removal of the Church from the world scene. Many passages relate to this point.

First, there's Daniel 7:25: "And he (i.e., the Beast) will speak out against the Most High and wear down the saints of the Highest One, and he will intend to make alterations in times and law; and they will be given into his hand for a time (Aramaic *'iddan*), times and half a time" (NASB). The "saints" *(qaddishin)* or Christian community will be under tyrannous oppression from the world dictator, the Beast, for 3½ years (for *'iddan* is the same term as that used of the seven-year madness of Nebuchadnezzar in Daniel 4:23, 32). Why not for a longer period? Very likely because they have been removed from the earthly scene, having endured the wrath of man, to be sure, but not the far greater horrors and agonies of the last 3½ years when the wrath of God will be visited upon the empire of the Beast.

Daniel 9:27 reads, "And he (i.e., the prince who is to come) will make a firm covenant with the many (a term for the community of believers, derived originally from Isaiah

53:11-12) for one week (i.e., seven years), but in the middle of the week he will put a stop to sacrifice and grain offering (a reference to the practice of public worship by latter-day believers); and on the wing of abominations will come one who makes desolate, even until a complete destruction . . ." It would seem that this world-ruler of the end times will at the beginning of the seven-year period consolidate his power by allaying the fears of those who might feel threatened by him. He will therefore conclude a religious concordat guaranteeing the rights of worship to all of his citizenry, including the Christian and Hebrew communions, until he has brought the religious establishment under complete control through his appointed underlings. Then he will move into the second stage of his master-strategy and suppress all freedom of thought and faith.

Like Hitler, he will attempt to coerce everyone to worship himself alone as the embodiment of the Divine upon earth.

Third, there's Daniel 12:7 which says, ". . . The angel swore by Him who lives forever that it would be for a time (Hebrew *mo'ed,* equivalent to Aramaic *'iddan),* times and half a time; and as soon as they finish shattering the power of the holy people, all these events (i.e., events leading up to the time of unparalleled tribulation and subsequent resurrection of the dead, Daniel 12:1-2) will be completed"

(NASB). The Beast, then, will resort to the most ruthless brutality in crushing all the resistance of Bible-believers and imposing his all-encompassing tyranny upon mankind by the midpoint of the seven years allotted him.

Daniel 12:11 states, "And from the time that the regular sacrifice is abolished (that is, all public worship of God is suppressed), and the abomination of desolation (i.e., the proclamation of the Beast himself as God incarnate, cf. II Thessalonians 2:3-4) is set up, there will be 1290 days (which would be twelve days more than 3½ years)." This would seem to indicate that about 3½ years (the second half, therefore, of the final seven-year period) would be the time allotted for the cult of the Beast, leaving the first 3½ years for the preliminary (or preabomination) phase.

In Revelation 11:2, the angel who is measuring the dimensions of the future temple is instructed not to measure the temple court, "for it has been given to the nations; and they will tread under foot the holy city for forty-two months." This seems to indicate the same second-half stage as the previous citation from Daniel 12:11, the brutal oppression of Jerusalem during the full fury of the great tribulation.

Revelation 12:14 declares that "the two wings of the great eagle were given to the woman (probably representing Israel, and the mother that had given birth to the

Messiah—no such flight to the wilderness was ever part of the Virgin Mary's experience), in order that she might fly into the wilderness to her place, where she was nourished for a time (Greek *kairon*, equivalent to *mo'ed* and *'iddan*) and times and half a time, from the presence of the serpent." This likewise seems to refer to the final half of the seven-year period, during which the tribulation saints (many of whom were converted Jews who have turned to Christ) will hide from persecution in the wilderness. Conceivably this might refer, however, to the earlier phase (i.e., the first 3½ years) since the rapture itself does not come clearly into view until Revelation 14. At any rate, the importance of a pivotal event in the midst of the final seven years is unmistakably implied.

I believe that the rapture also is mentioned in the Olivet discourse. Of course, more than one interpretation is possible when dealing with the question of the Olivet discourse (Matthew 24, Mark 13, Luke 21) and its bearing upon the rapture. There is no explicit reference to welcoming the Church into the presence of Christ prior to the final doom of Armageddon, and most advocates of the any-moment rapture question whether it is even alluded to in this prophetic message of Christ during Passion Week. Nevertheless it is highly significant that the same term for the *coming* of the Lord is employed in the Olivet discourse as is used in the rapture passage of I Thessalonians 4. Compare Matthew 24:27 ("For just as the lightning comes from the east, and flashes even to the west, so shall the coming—*parousia*—of the Son of Man be") and I Thessalonians 4:15 ("... we who are alive and remain until the coming—*parousia*—of the Lord"). Since the same word—and a rather unusual word at that—is used in both passages, it is fair to conclude that it refers to the same event.

Furthermore, it seems quite clear that Paul intends the rapture passage in I Thessalonians 4 to serve as an explication of the great day referred to in II Thessalonians 2:1: "Now we request you, brethren, with regard to the coming *(parousia)* of our Lord Jesus Christ, and our gathering together *(episynagoge)* to Him ..." It is highly significant that the verbal form of this *episynagoge* appears in Matthew 24:31: "And He will send forth His angels and they will gather together *(episynaxousin*, from *episynago)* His elect from the four winds, from one end of the sky to the other." The same distinctive term for the gathering of believers to meet the returning Lord appears in both passages, and in both cases it is an assembling of the entire Church which is implied, from all over the earth (the four winds and the regions of the sky are employed in the Old Testament to refer to the various climates and geographical regions associated with wind and sky).

The Olivet discourse seems therefore to make it clear that there will be a preliminary phase of the great tribulation (Matthew 24:21) of great intensity and resulting in great slaughter of the saints (verse 22) *prior to* (cf. verse 24) the sending forth of the angels to gather all believers together for the *parousia*, i.e. the rapture. Furthermore, the Lord Himself seems to lay great emphasis upon the fact that believers may recognize the approach of His *parousia* by the preliminary signs He has just described (verse 14—the spread of the Gospel to every nation; verse 15—the rise of the Beast, who will present himself as the abomination of desolation; etc.) and that they are therefore to be on guard as they observe them.

The indications of the imminent budding of a fig tree are furnished as an analogy to this (verses 32-33). This can hardly be restricted to a national conversion of post-rapture Israel alone, since the parallel passage in Luke 21:29 records that there was no restricted symbolism involving one species of tree alone (even if it could be conceded that the fig tree is symbolic of Israel only).

The rapture, then, is to take place after the fulfillment of certain predicted signs, and after the preliminary phase of the tribulation (the wrath of man) as described in Matthew 24:10-27. Nor does there seem to be much basis for the common supposition that it is to be a

49

secret rapture beheld only by the translated saints, for there is great display implied both by the great shout and the blast of the celestial trumpet (I Thessalonians 4:16; cf. Revelation 11:15; 14:2). It is difficult to imagine how this would escape the notice of mankind in general. In fact this stupendous theophany (Matthew 24:30: "the sign of the Son of Man will appear in the sky") may contribute much to the impact of the sudden disappearance of all believers from the world scene, resulting in the conversion of a large number of the rest of earth's population left behind by the rapture (cf. Revelation 7:9, 14).

It is usually believed by the advocates of an any-moment rapture at the commencement of the "final week," that the rapture itself is alluded to in Revelation 4:1: "After these things I (John) looked, and behold, a door standing open in heaven, and the first voice which I had heard, like the sound of a trumpet speaking with me, said, 'Come up here, and I will show you what must take place after these things.'"

The apostle John, all by himself (so far as the text states) is then lifted up, not merely to the clouds, but to heaven itself, where he sees the glorified Christ enthroned in royal splendor. But can this fairly be interpreted as agreeing with the specifications of I Thessalonians 4:16-17, where the Lord is described as coming down *from* heaven (rather than enthroned *in* heaven), and meeting the whole company of His saints (not just John alone) in the clouds (rather than up in glory)? There are too many discrepancies between the two passages to allow such an identification as plausible.

But when we turn to Revelation 14:14 we notice that Christ comes from heaven in a cloud, to the accompaniment of a loud voice from heaven. As we look back to 14:1 we see that He is accompanied by His faithful believers, represented by the 144,000 saints who proved true to him through every trial, and who are described as uncontaminated by spiritual adultery (being *parthenoi* or "virgins" who have not defiled themselves immorally with women—which has nothing to do with lawful marriage, commended by Scripture as "honorable in all"—Hebrews 13:4). The number 144,000 is probably symbolic: the factors are twelve times twelve (the Patriarchs, the Tribes and the Apostles were all twelve in number; cf. Ephesians 2:20; Revelation 21:12, 14), and 1000 represents the cube of ten, which figured as the measurements of the Holy of Holies in the Tabernacle, the number of perfect completion in the presence of God.

It should be observed that in Revelation 14:14-16 Jesus appears as the triumphant Son of Man, who has sent forth His angels to do the harvesting (as in Matthew 13:39, 41), casting the tares into a furnace of fire (Revelation

14:18). Observe that these tares are first gathered into bundles, then the wheat is gathered into His barn, as suggested by Matthew 13:30. As for the saints who accompany the Lamb, they are described as having been purchased "out of the earth" *(apo tes ges)*, according to Revelation 14:3, which suggests that they have been taken away from the place out of which they were purchased. This would seem appropriate to those who have been exalted from earth as a result of the rapture. They are seen as a company of "firstfruits" *(aparkhe)* up in heaven with the Lamb before the final phase of the "last days" even commences (as described in Revelation 16-18). As that grim time (the final agony of the unconverted world) descends upon the earth, this smaller number of redeemed believers (since firstfruits are always smaller than the main harvest itself) are up there in glory in the presence of the Lamb, prior to the final outbreak of the full fury of the Beast during the last 3½ years before Armageddon. And as J.O. Buswell points out *(Systematic Theology,* vol. 2, page 397), the 7th trumpet, referred to in Revelation 11:15-19, appears to announce rewards for the righteous dead (11:18), as well as the coming of the wrath of Almighty God. This may well be identical with the trumpet of the rapture mentioned in I Thessalonians 4:16.

Not only did Jesus put His return "immediately after the tribulation," but He made His return as unmistakable as a flash of lightning.

CHAPTER 4

JESUS IS COMING AGAIN: POSTTRIBULATION

BY ROBERT H. GUNDRY

In His great discourse on coming events (Matthew 24; Mark 13; Luke 21) Jesus spoke about a special time of "tribulation." Properly, that tribulation refers to persecution: "Then they will deliver you up to tribulation, and will kill you, and you will be hated by all nations on account of My name" (Matthew 24:9). However, the term has come to mean the period of time characterized by the unequalled persecution as well as the persecution itself.

Not only did Jesus put His return "immediately after the tribulation of those days" (Matthew 24:29), but He also made His immediately subsequent return as public and unmistakable as a flash of lightning (Matthew 24:27). Because Jesus has not returned with such display, the tribulation that He described has not yet occurred. Moreover, events of the prior tribulation are portrayed as recognizable at the time of occurrence: "when you see the abomination of desolation . . . standing in the holy place" (Matthew 24:15); "when you see all these things" (Matthew 24:33). Their unmistakability to the saints rules out a merely "possible" fulfillment already in the past or present time.

The command to flee into the mountains at the setting up of the abomination of desolation in the holy place, or Temple, and the difficulty of escape in winter or on a Sabbath (Matthew 24:20) is naturally limited to believers "in Judea" (Matthew 24:16), the immediate vicinity of the holy place with nearby mountains which have traditionally provided refuge for fugitives. And heavy winter rains would make travel into the mountainous wilderness of Judea difficult, as would also the lack of services to travelers on a Sabbath.

Nothing here implies that God has reinstituted the Mosaic law in the absence of the Church. As a matter of fact, it is the Antichrist, the coming prince, who will allow the Jewish people to practice Mosaic sacrifices, and then stop them from doing so (Daniel 9:26, 27). Jesus merely takes into consideration prevalent circumstances in Judean society for those disciples who will be living there at the time.

The reference to "the abomination of desolation which was spoken of through Daniel the prophet" lets us know that Jesus had in mind the seventieth week of Daniel 9:24-27, a period of seven years bisected in the middle by the erection of an image of the Antichrist (also called "the Beast" and "the man of lawlessness") in the Temple (see also Revelation 13:11-15 with II Thessalonians 2:3,4).

Because of the intensity of persecution, God will "cut short" those days (Matthew 24:22). The past tense, used in addition to the future tense concerning the cutting short, commonly appears in Biblical predictions, e.g., "He was wounded for our transgressions," written in Isaiah 53:5 long before the death of Christ. For that reason and for the reason that the number seven denotes completeness we can hardly think of God's originally planning a longer period which He will shorten to seven years. Jesus' statement that those days of the tribulation will be cut short makes sense only if God will mercifully keep the seven (or latter 3½) years from running their full course.

Deliverance will come somewhat prematurely, then, but none too soon. The elect will be gathered at Jesus' return right after the shortened tribulation (Matthew 24:29-31). Some will be "taken," others "left" (Matthew 24:40). Meanwhile, the elect are to watch for that event by watching for the events of the tribulation leading up to it: "when you see all these things [tribulation events just described], recognize that He is near, right at the door" (Matthew 24:33); "when these things begin to take place, straighten up and lift your heads, because your redemption is drawing near" (Luke 21:28). But though the saints will then know with certainty the general nearness of Jesus' return, the indeterminate cutting short of those days prevents any knowledge of the exact "day and hour" (Matthew 24:36).

Several days later in a promise to come again and receive believers to Himself (John 14:1-3), Jesus failed to distinguish that return from the one He had just put after the tribulation. And He said all these things to the disciples who formed the apostolic foundation of the Church (Ephesians 2:20). Did Paul supply any such missing information?

In I Thessalonians 4:13-18 Paul describes the descent of Christ and the catching up, or rapture, of resurrected and translated saints to the accompaniment of the archangel's voice and God's trumpet. Now Michael, the only archangel known in the Bible (Jude 9), appears elsewhere in connection with the resurrection only in Daniel 12:1-3, a passage generally agreed to deal with a resurrection after the tribulation.

In I Corinthians 15:52 Paul identifies the trumpet as "the last." This ties in with Jesus' having associated the gathering of the elect with "a great trumpet ... immediately after the tribulation" (Matthew 24:29-31). And John was yet to write of a final, seventh trumpet when "the kingdom of the world" at last becomes "the kingdom of our Lord," apparently at the close of the tribulation in view of the Antichrist's reign during that period (Revelation 11:15-19). Moreover, Paul gives no indication that Jesus will stop His descent for a lengthy stay "in the air," much less reverse His direction in a return to heaven. Rather, Paul uses an expression, "to meet," that in his day frequently referred to a welcoming party's going out of a city a little ways in order to greet a visiting dignitary and escort him immediately back into their city.

In I Thessalonians 5 Paul proceeds to tell the "brethren" they don't need information about the "times and epochs," not because no information is to be had but—as we learn from II Thessalonians 2:5—because he had told them while he was still with them. Therefore, the day of the Lord will not overtake "you" like a thief, he tells the Christians. "You" will be watching—and are exhorted to do so—with the result that the Lord's approach will be made very clear by the foretold preceding events.

Only on "them," the wicked, will the day of the Lord come "like a thief." Like those in Jeremiah's day who cried, "Peace, peace, when there is no peace," sudden destruction will come on them "while they are *saying* [not, when there will *be*], 'Peace and safety!' "—a hope, not a condition of fact. That destructive wrath will not strike the saved, however, for by virtue of their salvation in Christ they will have just risen to meet Him and accompany Him in His continued descent to "deal out retribution to those who do not know God and to those who do not obey the Gospel of our Lord Jesus" (II Thessalonians 1:8).

Significantly, Paul puts the "relief" of Christians "afflicted" by persecution "at the revelation of the Lord Jesus from heaven with His mighty angels in flaming fire" to "deal out" the above-mentioned "retribution" (II Thessalonians 1:6-10)—hardly a description of any event other than the coming of Christ in judgment at the close of the tribulation.

Then Paul writes that the Thessalonian church shouldn't think that the day of the Lord has already come. At least two obvious events must happen first: "the apostasy" and the revelation of the Antichrist, or "man of lawlessness" (II Thessalonians 2:1-4). Apostasy means rebellion. Paul further defines it as the Antichrist's attempt to displace God by "displaying himself as being God." Because all this will occur during the tribulation, we have to ask why Paul told the church to "be alert and sober" for the arrival of the day of the Lord (I Thessalonians 5:4-6) unless Christians will in fact live through the tribulational "apostasy" and revelation of "the man of lawlessness" which will "come first."

For the time being, something—or someone—restrains Antichrist's appearance (II Thessalonians 2:5-7). Tantalizingly, Paul refers to the restraint first as a thing, or abstraction, then as a person, but feels no need to make an identification because of his prior teaching within the church at Thessalonica. Does he mean the rule of law as concentrated in a governmental figure such as the reigning Caesar, in contrast to the Antichrist as a "man of lawlessness"? Or does God's Spirit, a grammatically impersonal word in Greek but personal in meaning so that it/He can be referred to either way—does the Spirit keep the Antichrist from appearing? Even if so, we have no indication that He does that through the Church's presence on earth rather than directly. After all, everybody has to agree—and does—that a huge number of saints of one kind or another will live on earth during the tribulation. It will take the ministry of the Spirit to make them both saints and witnesses in whom "it is the Holy Spirit" who speaks (Mark 13:11).

In any case the omission of an identification of the restrainer reduces us to guessing, hardly the kind of activity that establishes theological dogmas. Paul already has written clearly enough to indicate that Christians will observe the tribulational career of the Antichrist right up to the day of the Lord when Christ will come to crush that lawless persecutor and pretender to deity. As in exhortations of Jesus, we are to watch for His return in connection with signaling events of the tribulation.

Jesus has the last word in His Revelation to John of "the things which you have seen, and the things which are, and the things which shall take place after these things" (Revelation 1:19; compare 4:1). Does that mean that the future things concerning the tribulation and following (chapters 4-22) will take place after the present things concerning the Church (chapters 2 and 3)? Yes, but only in John's personal experience of receiving one vision after another, as is shown throughout Revelation by the repeated use of the phrase "after these things" for sequence of visions and sights within visions: "after these things I looked" (7:9; see also 15:5; 18:1; 19:1).

And the sequence of John's visions doesn't necessarily correspond to historical sequence; for example, long after the introduction of the tribulation, chapter 12 opens with the *birth* of Christ! In other words, the fact that John saw visions concerning the tribulation after he received messages for the seven churches in western Asia Minor says nothing one way or the other as to whether the tribulation falls into the last part of the age of the Church.

John is caught up to heaven in Revelation 4:1,2. But that was only his personal experience for the reception of a vision there. Later, we see John back on earth— in the tribulational section (10:1; 11:1ff; 13:1; 18:1; 20:1; 21:2). And nobody says that John's movements represent a commuting of the

Church between heaven and earth during the tribulation.

In heaven John finds twenty-four elders crowned and clothed in white robes. But even the demonic locusts (9:7) and the woman Israel (21:1) wear crowns. And Christians still on earth and martyrs still unresurrected may wear white robes (3:18; 6:11). Yet there has been no rapture for any of them. We know only that the twenty-four elders help lead the heavenly worship of God.

The term "church" never appears in the great central section of Revelation where John describes the tribulation. But the knife has a double edge. Many of the scenes are set in heaven (4:1-5:14; 6:9-11; 7:9-8:5; 11:15-12:12; 15:2-16:1; 19:1-10). John doesn't mention "church" in those scenes either. But he does repeatedly refer to saints still on earth. In the absence of even the slightest description of a return of Christ until the close of the tribulation (19:11-16), we can only conclude that those saints make up the last generation of the Church for which Christ has not yet returned.

Though persecuted and subject to the effects of human wickedness (as are Christians of every generation), those saints will receive protection from divine wrath, particularly that poured out at the very end in connection with the final battle of Armageddon in Palestine. (See especially 15:1; 16:1-21. Fuller study will show that divine wrath appears only at the ends of the series of plagues and that each series closes not until the end of the tribulation.)

A promise of such protection appears in Revelation 3:10: "I will keep you from the hour of testing." "Keep" means "guard" and "from" means "out from within." The only other time these two words occur together, they express an idea totally opposed to removal from the earthly sphere of danger: "I do not ask Thee to take them out of the world, but to keep them from the evil one" (John 17:15). Naturally, guarding makes sense only within the sphere of danger with the result of coming successfully out of the time of danger.

Therefore we needn't look on the 144,000 as God's witnesses in the absence of the Church. John never assigns them that role anyway (see Revelation 7:1-8; 14:1-4). If they don't represent the Church itself as the new people of God, they probably represent orthodox Jews who, though not yet believing in Christ, refuse to worship the Antichrist (Revelation 12). God would then preserve them for repentance and faith at the end, when they see their Messiah descending with the just-raptured Church, and also for their becoming the nucleus of Christ's subsequent kingdom on earth (Romans 11:25-27; Zechariah 12:10-13:1; Zephaniah 13:8-13).

The rapture itself appears under the figure

of a harvest gathered by "one like a son of man," golden-crowned and "sitting on a cloud" (Revelation 14:14-16; compare 1:7; Matthew 24:30, 31; Acts 1:9-11). That harvest leads right into another harvest, that of the wicked at the final battle of Armageddon (Revelation 14:17-20). As a result, the vultures will feed on "the great supper of God" (Revelation 19:15-21). But like bridegroom and bride (and the bride includes Israel as well as the Church, according to Revelation 21:9-14), Christ and the saints will victoriously celebrate at "the marriage supper of the Lamb," which John delays mentioning until he has described Jesus' return after the tribulation (Revelation 19:6ff). He similarly fails to place the first resurrection at any other time (Revelation 20:4-6).

In the light of all this scriptural evidence, it shouldn't surprise us that in the history of interpretation nobody thought of separating Christ's return into two phases and making the first phase an "out" for the Church—until the late 1820's (see Robert H. Gundry. *The Church and the Tribulation,* Zondervan, 1973). Neither should it surprise us that more and more students of the Bible are going back to the early church's way of looking for the blessed hope as the culmination of a series of recognizably significant events during and immediately after a future period of tribulation.

The Bible simply does not teach a second coming of Christ for the Church, followed some seven years later by a third coming for the world.

CHAPTER 5

JESUS IS COMING AGAIN: PASTTRIBULATION

BY J. BARTON PAYNE

The "rapture rupture" debate zeroes in on three major issues. *First is the imminence of Christ's return* and our being caught up into the clouds to meet Him. This is the issue on which pretribulationists have made their point. A thing that is imminent is defined in Webster's Dictionary as "threatening to occur immediately." While it would be rash to claim that Jesus' second coming must be soon, or perhaps today, it looks equally unwise to deny (as posttribulationists do) that it *could* be today. The Bible says, "Watch! For ye know not when the time is" (Mark 13:33, 35, 37).

The posttribulationist, of course, quickly asserts that the New Testament's command to watch does not always entail the imminent appearing of Christ. True enough. In I Thessalonians 5:6, to watch means to "be alert" (NASB), to be spiritually awake in reference to our conduct.

In Acts 1:6, when the disciples were looking

for the restoration of the kingdom to Israel, Jesus told them of an intervening responsibility: First, they must be witnesses for Him in far parts of the earth (v. 8). Note clearly, however: The fact that the apostles had a postponed hope in their day does not mean that what they wrote demands a postponed hope in our day. The apostle Peter, who knew that he had to die before Christ would return (John 21:19), could warn others that "the end is at hand" (I Peter 4:7). Again, in Luke 21:28, the command for watchfulness, which Jesus gave His disciples, included their looking for a chain of events, only the last of which would be His visible appearing (verses 25-27).

But in some other passages none of these explanations will do. For example, in Luke 12:35-40 He said, "Be like men that wait for their Lord . . . that when he cometh and knocketh, they may open unto him immediately . . . Be ye therefore ready, for the Son of man cometh at an hour when ye think not." Jesus says we are to watch, not just over our own conduct (true though this is) but for His knock, not in the light of postponement but for a fulfillment when we think not; not for a chain of events but specifically for His coming. We are waiting for the Lord who will break in like a thief (v. 38). I can only have sympathy for the posttribulationist whose preconceptions force him to say things

like, "Whatever this means, it cannot involve...
an any-moment, unexpected return of Christ"
(George E. Ladd, *The Blessed Hope,* p. 111).

*The second issue is that of the unity of
Christ's return,* namely, that it takes place all
at one time and not in two stages separated by
the great tribulation. This is where
posttribulationists have made their strong
point. The Bible simply does not teach (as do
pretribulationists) a second coming of Christ
for the Church followed some seven years later
by a "third coming" for the world. In Titus
2:12-13 the Christian's hope is the Lord's
glorious appearing, His final revealing (I
Corinthians 1:7, NASB). In II Thessalonians
2:6-8, the "rest" granted to the Church occurs
only at that point where Jesus is revealed from
heaven, with His mighty angels, in flaming
fire, taking vengeance on those who do not
know God.

In Revelation 20:4-5 the vindication of the
saints is placed at the start of the millennium
(v. 2). Because this is called the "first"
resurrection, it could hardly be preceded by
some other "really first" resurrection.
Therefore, how could the one in I
Thessalonians 4:14-17 be earlier and different
from it? In I Corinthians 15:51-54 the change in
body (and the rapture) of believers alive at the
time of Christ's return is located "at the last
trump," when "death is swallowed up in
victory." The latter phrase is a quote from

Isaiah 25:8, belonging at the outset of the millennial kingdom (v.6). And the trumpet in the former phrase could hardly be followed by some other "really last" trumpet—as though the one in Matthew 24:31 were later and different from it.

These elements form one, unified event. (See Payne, *The Prophecy Map of World History,* Harper and Row, 1974.) To put it in another way, let's ask ourselves this question: When the saints meet their Lord in the air at His descent from heaven (I Thessalonians 4:17), who turns around and goes back? Not Christ who seems to continue right on to the Mount of Olives to set up His kingdom (Zechariah 14:5)—but rather we who form His escort (compare the same sort of "going out to meet Him" in Matthew 25:6, Acts 28:15). And so shall we ever be with the Lord (I Thessalonians 4:17).

My sympathy is with the pre-(and mid-) tribulationists, whose preconceptions force them to locate the rapture separately, some time before Christ's appearing at the close of the tribulation *(The New Scofield Reference Bible,* p. 1250), when not a syllable in the Bible teaches such a disjunction.

Well, then, what are those preconceptions which force both pretribs and midtribs into their respective dilemmas? They can be summed up under the third major issue in the debate, the *futurism that both approaches have introduced* into the picture of Christ's return.

It's not just that His second coming lies in the future: everybody agrees on this. The issue we label futurism is whether long drawn-out events—events that take several years and that haven't happened yet, such as a rebuilding of the Temple in Jerusalem—have to occur before Jesus Christ can come back. The situation can be laid out, along with our other two issues, in the form of a triangle:

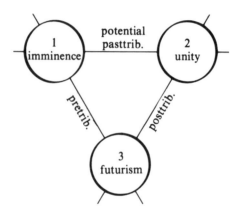

(see Payne, *The Imminent Appearing of Christ,* p. 157).

A straight line, however, can be drawn through only two of its points. For example, the interpreter who draws his line in favor of imminence and yet believes in prolonged futuristic antecedents to Christ's second advent has to deny its unity. Thus the pretribulationist divides up the Lord's return, makes part of it (the rapture part) imminent, and puts the rest after a future tribulation. We call this the dispensational position, since it began only in 1830 with J.N. Darby's acceptance of Margaret MacDonald's revelation in Port Glasgow of a dispensationally divided return (see D. MacPherson, *The Unbelievable Pre-Trib Origin,* Heart of America Bible Society, 1973).

Or, as another example, the interpreter who draws his line in favor of unity and yet accepts futuristic antecedents to the second advent has to deny its imminence. This is especially the position of former dispensationalists who have reacted against its dividing up of events, while continuing to retain some of its futurism. George Ladd, for instance, refers to the seventieth seven-year week of Daniel as still future and thus questions imminency, saying, "In the middle of the week Antichrist has broken his covenant with Israel. In such a day any believers would know almost the precise time of Christ's return at the end of the three-and-one-half years" (*The Blessed Hope*, p. 111; see also Robert H. Gundry's new book, *The Church and the Tribulation,* pp. 43, 189).

The real question, however, is whether today's Christian is limited in his choice to these two possibilities. Is he indeed caught on the horns of a dilemma so that he has to give up either the Bible's teaching on imminence or its teaching on unity? (The midtribber, by the way, draws his line through futurism alone and has to give up both the others.)

Isn't there some other way to draw a line and include both? Of course there is, if you are willing to reexamine the necessity of futurism. There *is* a harmony of truth: it's the option of pasttribulationism (we might more accurately call it "potentially pasttribulation"). That is, Jesus could come back today (imminency); He will both rapture the church and set up His millennial kingdom (unity); and this will prove we have already had all the tribulation that is required (no more futurism).

How can this be? Let's look at the lines of possible approach. They will suggest some methods that I have found to deal with the problems.

The first approach is this: Some prophecies that have been treated as future antecedents to Christ's return may already have been fulfilled and so are already past. For example, Ezekiel's temple (Ezekiel 40-46) was intended to have been rebuilt by the prophet's contemporaries (see 43:10-11: and notice the distinctively B.C. features in vv. 20 and 27): they didn't, but that was not Ezekiel's fault. Or about Daniel's seventieth week (Daniel 9:24-27), the most natural reading seems to be this: that what followed the prophet's sixty-ninth period of seven years (ending with the anointing of Israel's Messiah, v. 25, i.e., at His baptism, in

A.D. 26) was the prophet's seventieth period of seven years. During this time, the Messiah confirmed His covenant to Israel and, after three-and-one-half years, was cut off and ended the sacrificial system of the Old Testament (assuming that v. 27 recapitulates v. 26, just as vv. 25-26 recapitulate v. 24). After all, what's the point in having seventy weeks if they do not run consecutively and add up to exactly seventy?

Then there is the great tribulation itself. Many popular interpreters confuse the tribulation (as in Revelation 6:9-11) with the period of heavenly phenomena which Scripture designates as "the wrath of God" (6:12-17). The two shouldn't be confused. The tribulation comes before the wrath (see Matthew 24:29), and it consists of the final persecutions by the Antichrist (see Daniel 12:1 or Revelation 7:14).

We may already have had, right now, the total of this persecution intended, for we in our sheltered little part of North America form a unique minority out of the world's population. If we were living in China or Chile, in Czechoslovakia or Cuba, in Armenia or Vietnam, we might well wonder if things could be worse. Several remarkably well-qualified candidates for the office of Antichrist are already revealed in this twentieth-century world (which has produced more martyrs for Jesus than any other period in church history).

It would take only the coming of Christ to show which one would actually lead the opposition to Him, suffer destruction, and thus be the Bible's man of sin (see Payne's *Biblical Prophecy for Today,* Harper and Row, 1974).

This, it should be noted, has been the classical position of the church through the ages. The early fathers felt that Caesar could be the Antichrist; the Reformers felt it could be the Pope. Only since Darby, has any significant segment of the church looked for Daniel's seventieth week at a time other than in the first century (See Froom, *The Prophetic Faith of our Fathers,* I:278, 890).

A second line of approach assumes that some prophecies are indeed future but do not really fit into the category of future antecedents because they are too far in the future; that is, they occur after our Lord's appearing. Matters like the marriage supper of the Lamb (Isaiah 25:6-7, Revelation 19:7-9) or the battle of Armageddon (Daniel 11:45, Revelation 16:16) have to happen after Christ comes. They occur because of His presence.

The third approach puts some prophecies in the future. They do precede the appearing of Christ. Here we should include certain elements of the wrath of God, such as the great earthquake and the sun being darkened (Matthew 24:29, cf. the first four trumpets and bowls of God's wrath in Revelation 8 and 16:1-9). But as long as the Lord protects His people from these things (and He does: I Thessalonians 5:9; Revelation 7:1-3), and as long as they are restricted to events that last only a few minutes (and this is all they do: Luke 21:28), then such matters do not invalidate the Church's imminent hope. In fact, they provide just enough interval to get the car parked, the one driven by that Christian who told the hitch-hiker, "Ride at your own risk, I'm going up in the rapture."

Where then does this leave you? Let me suggest two guidelines.

As far as the debate goes, be negative. Don't listen to a prophecy teacher's strong arguments—no matter how convincing. Instead, push him to the wall where he's weakest. Make the pretribulationist account for those Bible passages that teach the unity of our Lord's return. Make the posttribulationist account for those Bible passages that teach His imminence. And make the (potentially) past-rapturist account for those Bible passages that teach futurism. Then pick the position that seems least bad.

But as far as the faith goes, be positive. Treat men as Christians who have accepted Jesus Christ as their Lord (Acts 16:31); and treat men as church officers who accept the Bible as His inerrant word (Titus 1:9). We should never read a teaching elder out of fellowship because of Bible-based differences of interpretation over the tribulation.

And let us live soberly, righteously and godly in this present world, looking for that blessed hope, and the glorious appearing of the great God and our Savior Jesus Christ ... that we may have confidence and not be ashamed before Him at His coming (Titus 2:12,13; I John 2:28).

A number stamped on each person to make buying and selling easier, persecution of charismatic Catholics, a revival as powerful as Pentecost—these events plus many more are predicted in books and cassettes on the "end times."

APPENDIX A
LEARN MORE ABOUT TOMORROW

"A friend who was with the Northwest National Bank," says Willard Cantelon in his book, *The Day the Dollar Dies* (Logos; 149 pp; $2.50 paper), "recently spoke of the progress being made in the laboratories in developing an invisible, nontoxic ink which would be tattooed on man's flesh, invisible in normal light, but clearly legible in a special light . . .

"Imagine, life without money . . . No more checkbooks to balance . . . There was only one small prerequisite: for such a system to work, it would require every man to have a number . . . As the prophet had predicted almost two thousand years previously, 'No man might buy or sell, save he that had . . . the number' (Revelation 13:7,16,17)."

Cantelon is referring, of course, to the number system to be set up by the predicted Antichrist—the one who insists that everyone in the world bow down and worship him.

Cantelon's book is thought-provoking and well worth its cost.

Another suspense-filled book is David Wilkerson's *The Vision* (Spire; 143 pp; $1.50 paper), which recounts a message which he says he received from the Lord in April 1973.

The next few years, writes Wilkerson, will be among the most prosperous in the history of mankind—then the lean years will come in the form of a major recession. Earthquakes will plague the U.S. in unexpected places. Huge hailstones will hit the earth, and there will be strange signs in the sky.

Evil will run rampant, Wilkerson says. TV will feature toplessness; pornography. Homosexuality will pose a threat to human life, as homosexual gangs roam the country.

There will be special persecution for charismatic Catholics, but "renewed" Christians will come out from all denominations for fellowship, "based not on speaking with tongues but centered on the Father and His Son, Jesus Christ," Wilkerson says.

Neither Wilkerson nor Cantelon declares where he stands on the tribulation (pre-, mid- or posttrib), but a third book, *Satan in the Sanctuary,* is definitely pretrib. Written by Thomas S. McCall and Zola Levitt, this slim volume (Moody; 120 pp; $3.95; $1.95 paper) gives some interesting facts about the diggings underneath the Dome of the Rock, the Temple site. Although the authors were able to interview only two eyewitnesses of the actual diggings, the authors discovered that (1) the ancient weights and measurements, so necessary to a restored Temple, had been found, and (2) these new findings and others, are being used to educate the Jewish people in Temple worship.

All this, say the authors, shows that a rebuilt Temple is a definite possibility in the near future. This, of course, is a harbinger of Christ's return.

Do Jews also look for the Messiah? Yes, says Kurt Koch in his exciting book, *The Coming One* (Kregel, $1). He quotes a journalist who said, "The war last summer (the 1967 Six-Day War) achieved more in the space of a few days than 500 missionaries could have achieved in a lifetime." One young Jewish soldier told Koch, "We are the last generation." And the Jews know, Koch says, that God helped them in the war. Fascinating examples are cited: Arab prisoners related how they had lost the will to fight when they saw soldiers dressed in white fighting for the Israelies, but the Israelies knew nothing of the incident; at a kibbutz, the leader decided to fire some flares then "run for it"—but the flares ignited a nearby corn field and the Syrians fled in panic; and on another occasion as a detachment of Israeli soldiers passed Abraham's tomb, they saw an old man, dressed in white, praying with arms uplifted.

As they approached him, he disappeared. What did it mean? Who was he? This is a heartwarming, encouraging book.

Although not strictly a book on end-time prophecy, ". . . And There Will Be Famines," by Larry Ward (Regal; 114 pp; $1.25 paper) has an apocalyptic "feel," and is loaded with predictions about the problem of hunger in the world—a problem, Ward says, which will grow to gigantic proportions as our population reaches 7.5 billion in the year 2000!

In Signs of the Times (Baker; 126 pp; $1.25 paper), author A. Skevington Wood says, "Before the return of Christ we may expect . . . a revival as powerful as Pentecost itself and much more widespread. It will be a time when God's people seek Him, and He comes and rains salvation on them (Hosea 10:12.)" Wood also has interesting comments on coming famines, earthquakes and other disasters.

Did you ever wonder where Scofield got his idea of a "secret" rapture of Christians? The story, as unfolded by Dave MacPherson in The Unbelieveable Pre-Trib Origin (Heart of America Bible Society; 123 pp; $4 paper), will intrigue you. If you're a pretribber, it might even make you angry. But MacPherson has a lot of documentation, he says, to prove that the pretrib view originated from a woman's prophetic "utterance" (as a result of the gift of tongues) in 1830.

S.I. McMillen, M.D., also has some

interesting observations in *Discern These Times* (Revell; 192 pp; $4.95). A study guide ($2.95 paper) adds additional insights. As Harold John Ockenga says in the introduction, some of the conclusions are "not so ready of proof," but each is stimulating. For example, McMillen believes that the rider of the white horse in Revelation 6 could be the United Nations. On the other hand, he believes Christians will have to suffer "the wrath of man" but not "the wrath of God," so he places the rapture at the sound of the last or seventh trumpet.

Interesting thoughts about the coming Antichrist are given in *What on Earth Is God Doing,* by Renald E. Showers (Loizeaux; 128 pp; $1.59 paper), which consists mainly of an overview of the conflict between good and evil, beginning in Genesis. "As a result of the current philosophy that man is evolving toward deification or man-godhood, the world is being conditioned for this kind of worship (of the Antichrist). Because of Antichrist's supernatural powers, it will be easy for the world to conclude that he is the ultimate product of evolution; therefore, he should be worshiped as the representative of what man is becoming—deity," Showers says.

Although the bulk of *The Last Chapter* (Living Books; 285 pp; $1.25 paper) is an autobiography of A.W. Rasmussen, Lutheran-turned-Pentecostal, the last portion of the book gives the author's interesting reaction to a newspaper headline. Rasmussen was in Canada at the time, and the headline stated, "Israel is a nation for the first time in 2,000 years." As he saw it, he remembered a passage in Hosea 6:1,2—"Come, and let us return unto the Lord; for he hath torn, and he will heal us; he hath smitten, and he will bind us up. After two days will he revive us; in the third day he will raise us up, and we shall live in his sight." Two days. Two thousand years. Suddenly Rasmussen remembered II Peter 3:8: "But, beloved, be not ignorant of this one thing, that one day is with the Lord as a thousand years, and a thousand years as one day."

Many predictions also are given by Charles C. Ryrie in *The Bible and Tomorrow's News* (Victor; 190 pp; $1.25). "If we are living today near the . . . beginning of the tribulation," Ryrie says, "we may expect to see certain trends in relation to the nation Israel. (1) Her ties with the West will grow stronger until, at the beginning of the tribulation, Israel and the West will conclude a mutual assistance treaty. (2) We will see Egypt continue to be an independent and important nation. (3) Russia will continue to influence the Middle East, most likely through the Arab states of that area. (4) The climax will be an invasion of Palestine, for since Israel will choose to align herself with the West, this will be the only way Russia can take her over. But God will intervene and will bring a spectacular judgment on Russia, resulting in her complete defeat."

Prophecy for Today (Zondervan; 231 pp; $1.50 paper), first published in 1961, is now in its fourteenth printing. Written by J. Dwight Pentecost, it not only explains the book of Revelation (from a pretrib viewpoint), but also explains Israel's title deed to Palestine, the meaning of Daniel's image and the federated states of Europe, and many other puzzling events of "the last days." In a similar book, *Before the Last Battle Armageddon,* Arthur E. Bloomfield describes the dramatic prophetic events about to happen on this planet. From Bethany Fellowship (192 pp; $2.25 paper), this also is from the pretrib viewpoint, and has maps, charts and listings.

An altogether different approach to eschatology is given by George Eldon Ladd in *The Presence of the Future* (Eerdmans; 370 pp; $4.50 paper). In it he examines the "Kingdom of God" as "a present reality in Jesus' mission," not only as an eschatological blessing.

And where does the U.S. fit into all of this? Not all authors discuss this subject, but some have strong viewpoints. For example, in *Maranatha* (published by Hamilton; 124 pp; $1.50 paper) author Gavin Hamilton says, "the prophetic words give us the inescapable conviction that Great Britain and her colonies, with the U.S. of America, shall be in closest collaboration in the end-time to give fullest support to the revived Roman Empire—which shall be under the indirect sway of the Papacy, or Babylon, the one-world church (Revelation 17). She shall appoint a dictator to assume full political control in her determination to offset the advances of communism coming from the North and East."

These, of course, are highlights from only a few of the many books on prophecy. As you've undoubtedly noticed, most are inexpensive; so even if you don't agree with everything each author says, buy as many as you can, and add some from the list which follows. But above all, read what God's Word says about all of these things.

APPENDIX B

MORE BOOKS ABOUT PROPHECY— PLUS BOOKLETS, CHARTS AND CASSETTES

THE REVELATION; by Arno C. Gaebelein; Loizeaux; $3.50. The Revelation is a book of prophecy, "capstone of the entire revelation of God, without which the Bible would be an unfinished book. We find in its pages the consummation of the great prophecies which were given by the Prophets of God in Old Testament times," says the author.

SIGNS OF CHRIST'S COMING; by Carl Armerding; Moody; 126 pp; $.50 paper. This prophetic study discusses the events and the return of Christ that will reverse the world situation. It focuses attention on the parables of Matthew 25, the statements of John, Acts and the Pauline epistles on Christ's return as Son of man.

BRIEF OUTLINES OF THINGS TO COME; Compiled by Theodore H. Epp; Moody; 128 pp; $.95. A detailed summary of what we may expect according to God's prophetic Word. Chapters on the restoration of Palestine, the great prophecy of the seventy weeks, the rapture and the first resurrection, the tribulation, Daniel's seventieth week, rewards, Christ's judgment of the nations, the millennium, doomsday and the future state.

WILL MAN SURVIVE?; by J. Dwight Pentecost; Moody; 208 pp; $1.95. Dwight Pentecost answers questions concerning the future of man's existence, centering his approach around the end times, the tribulation, the millennium and heaven.

THE LORD'S COMING; by C.H. Mackintosh; Moody; 118 pp; $.50 paper. Following a brief but important introduction, Mackintosh launches into a carefully charted course on the Lord's second coming. Proof of Christ's return, the two resurrections, the judgment, the Jewish remnant and Christendom's apostasy, the ten virgins, and the talents, the great parenthesis—each important truth receives reverent examination in this study of God's prophetic Word.

PROPHECY INTERPRETED; by John P. Milton; Augsburg; 150 pp; $2.95 paper. Do we live in the "last times," as many religious movements now declare? Are there "signs" in history which provide clues for seeing into the future? These and other timely questions are given serious attention in this book.

THE FUTURE OF THE GREAT PLANET EARTH; by Richard S. Hanson; Augsburg; 128 pp; $2.95 paper. The author emphasizes that the Bible is the story of God and his people, and the prophetic sections of the Bible are the communicators—bringing today's Christians words of caution, judgment, promise and hope. Only a misuse of the Bible, Hanson warns, can yield frightening references to modern nations and future events.

THE BIBLICAL DOCTRINE OF HEAVEN; by Wilbur M. Smith; Moody; 317 pp; $4.95. This work includes extensive footnotes, three appendixes and what may well be the most complete bibliography on the subject of heaven in the English language. Text, author and subject indexes make the information contained in this volume easily accessible.

REVELATION VISUALIZED; by Gary Cohen and Salem Kirban; Moody; 484 pp; $8.95. This book is written so that even the person with no Bible knowledge can understand. Verse-by-verse it gives commentary by Dr. Gary Cohen and background information by Salem Kirban. To further aid understanding, there are over 200 photographs, charts and diagrams explaining the points presented by the authors.

PROPHETIC PROBLEMS WITH ALTERNATE SOLUTIONS; by Clarence E. Mason; Moody; 192 pp; $4.95. Dr. Mason compiles the best of his writings on prophetic issues giving alternate solutions to controversial passages. Mason takes each problem individually and carefully presents what he considers a logical and more helpful approach than existing solutions.

CIVILIZATION'S LAST HURRAH; by Gary G. Cohen; Moody; 256 pp; $4.95. With scientific precision, terror, and all-too-real believability, the characters Tensing, Stradford, Oliver, and Rothchild move through the most chilling of days; Noah Days, Ten Horns, Invasion from the North, Fire in the Mountains, War, Famine, Martyrs, Cosmic Shakings, Bloody Seas, Locusts and Horsemen, Assassinations, the Israel Confrontation, Razed Cathedrals, Fire, and the horrifying climax of it all—Armageddon! Every man and woman alive fights with every human intellect and skill against the ultimate enemy—death.

PROPHECY AND THE SEVENTIES; by Charles Lee Feinberg; Moody; 256 pp; $4.95; $1.25 paper. Divided into four parts, this book covers Christ, the Church, Israel, and the nations—all in relationship to prophetic Scriptures. Vitalizing the discussion is a fresh application to today's situation.

THE END TIMES; by Herman A. Hoyt; Moody; 256 pp; $2.50 paper. *The End Times* is a thorough, well-documented treatise of premillennial, pretribulation eschatology, with consideration given to conflicting viewpoints. Included in this study are Christ's second coming (and its relationship to the church and the Antichrist), the resurrections and divine judgments.

A THIEF IN THE NIGHT; by Jim Grant; Moody; 128 pp; $1.50 paper. *A Thief in the Night* is an expansion of the script from the Mark IV Pictures production "A Thief in the Night." It is the dramatic story of what will happen to those who are not taken at the rapture.

PROPHECY MADE PLAIN FOR TIMES LIKE THESE; by Carl Johnson; Moody; 288 pp; $5.95. What place does Bible prophecy have in the analysis of our world situation? This question is central in *Prophecy Made Plain.* The book emphasizes God's predictions for the world and compares them to the current headlines—with some frightening conclusions.

QUESTIONS FREQUENTLY ASKED ME ON PROPHECY; by Salem Kirban; Moody; 64 pp; $1.95. This book takes a comprehensive look at coming events, with the help of charts, timetables, and photographs of current events, including a 17-page chart of specific prophecies Christ fulfilled in His life and death. Throughout, the author analyzes individual questions and points in light of the total picture of prophetic truth.

JESUS' PROPHETIC SERMON; by Walter K. Price; Moody; 160 pp; $4.95. Author Price takes the Olivet discourse and writes it on the front page of our lives. He shows the relevance between what goes on today and the words of the greatest Prophet.

THE KINGDOM OF GOD VISUALIZED; by Ray E. Baughman; Moody; 286 pp; $5.95. This book spotlights the kingdom program of God from Genesis to Revelation. It gives an extensive but simple overview of the coming, eternal kingdom of Jesus Christ.

THE RETURN OF JESUS CHRIST; by Rene Pache; Moody; 448 pp; $5.95. paper. Dr. Pache has taken up all the main themes of prophecy: Jesus as our hope; signs of His return; nations at the end of time; the four empires of Daniel; Satan, the Antichrist, and the False Prophet; Israel and her future; the millennium.

THE TRIBULATION PEOPLE; by Arthur Katterjohn with Mark Fackler; Creation House; $3.50. A fascinating, in-depth search of end-time Scriptures designed to help the reader discover which view is correct: pretribulation, midtribulation, pasttribulation. Katterjohn teaches at Wheaton (Ill.) College.

THERE'S A NEW WORLD COMING; by Hal Lindsey; Vision House; 308 pp; $4.95. An "effort to tell a mysteriously complicated saga" (of the book of Revelation) as a "simple, exciting story."

THE COMING ANTICHRIST; by Walter K. Price; Moody; 250 pp; $4.95. In this discussion of the Antichrist, Price examines first the history of attempts made to pinpoint him—concentrating on the Seleucid ruler, Antiochus IV, who was a type of Antichrist. The remaining sections discuss the various characteristics and names attributed to the Antichrist in Daniel and in the New Testament.

THE MOST REVEALING BOOK OF THE BIBLE: MAKING SENSE OUT OF REVELATION; by Vernard Eller; Eerdmans; 323 pp; $3.95 paper. Writing primarily for laymen, Eller avoids giving a lot of background information that doesn't contribute to an understanding of the book's message. The goal of this commentary is to determine the meaning of Revelation as a whole, and not just the small meanings of individual verses.

JESUS AND ISRAEL; by Carmen Benson; Logos; 189 pp; $.95. An interpretation of the Old Testament dreams and visions, plus the prophecies fulfilled by Jesus' coming. The dreams and visions related in Scripture teach us a great deal about how God works in the affairs of human beings.

THE EARTH'S END; by Carmen Benson; Logos; 152 pp; $.95 paper. This book is an interpretation of New Testament dreams and visions, and a look at the future through Biblical prophecy. Benson narrates events that are soon to happen, and tells how to avoid fear and panic.

THE LATE GREAT PLANET EARTH; by Hal Lindsey; Zondervan; 192 pp; paper, $2.25; cloth, $3.95. A runaway bestseller on the pretribulation view of the Second Coming of Jesus.

SEEDS OF CONFLICT; by Charles DeLoach; Logos; 100 pp; $4.95, $2.50 paper. Charles DeLoach gives an absorbing look at the sources and consequences of the Yom Kippur war. He describes the course of the conflict, and then takes you behind the scenes to explore the Biblical origins of the longstanding and bitter enmity between the Arab and the Jew.

THE VISIONS AND PROPHECIES OF ZECHARIAH; by David Baron; Kregel Publications; 555 pp; $6.95. The author's object is first of all to explain as fully as possible the great Messianic prophecies in this book, and secondly, to unfold and emphasize the great and solemn prophetic events which center around the land and people of Israel.

THE COMING PRINCE; by Sir Robert Anderson; Kregel Publications; 304 pp; $4.50. Anderson expounds on the prophecy of Daniel's Seventy Weeks concerning the Antichrist. He also deals with the prophecies of Daniel, Christ and John.

DANIEL; by Arno C. Gaebelein; Kregel Publications; 212 pp; $3.95. This chapter by chapter commentary is considered a key to the visions and prophecies of the book of Daniel.

THE HISTORIES AND PROPHECIES OF DANIEL; by G.H. Lang; Kregel Publications; 224 pp; $4.95. This book is a contribution to the study of Daniel, with special treatment given to the historical chapters. Lang also interprets the more obviously prophetic parts of Daniel, and looks into Ezekiel and the Antichrist in the appendixes.

A COMMENTARY ON THE REVELATION OF JOHN; by George E. Ladd; Eerdmans; 296 pp; $6.95. Beginning with a brief introduction, Ladd discusses the subject of authorship; the date and historical setting of Revelation; and the various methods of interpretation (Preterist, Historical, Idealist and Futurist) that have been applied to the book throughout history.

REVELATION ILLUSTRATED AND MADE PLAIN; by Tim F. LaHaye; Family Life Seminars

Publications; 449 pp; $4.95. This is a practical treatment of Revelation that everyone can understand. It combines an artist's concept of each symbol in the book, together with charts and diagrams of the events being prophesied.

THE REVELATION OF ST. JOHN; by C. Leon Morris; Eerdmans; 263 pp; $2.25. In this introduction and commentary, Dr. Morris attempts to explain the significance of its symbolism, and show the bearing of its message on living Christianity today.

THE BOOK OF REVELATION; by Louis T. Talbot; Eerdmans; 254 pp; $2.95. The symbolic language used in Revelation is often given as a reason for neglecting it. Dr. Talbot tells us that within the Word itself we are given the key to the symbols used, so that "those who neglect it are without excuse."

INTERPRETING REVELATION; by Merrill C. Tenney; Eerdmans; 202 pp; $4.50. This study is built on the thesis that Revelation has a definite message for those to whom it was first written, and that the meaning which they found should be the initial clue to its interpretation.

THE WAR WE CAN'T LOSE; by Henry Jacobsen; Victor Books; 96 pp; $.95 paper. This book is a clear look at Revelation, today's lifestyle, and the ages-long war between God and Satan.

GOD'S PLAN OF THE AGES; by Louis T. Talbot; Eerdmans; 199 pp; $2.25. This book is the outline of God's plan from the beginning of Genesis to the close of Revelation. The prophecies of Daniel are expounded in detail, as are those of Revelation.

THE GHOST OF HAGAR; by George Otis; Time-Light Books; 126 pp; $1.95. This book puts you right there in Israel's fourth "War of Atonement." The practical significance of current Jewish "happenings" will come into focus as we see that Israel is God's pivot at this moment when time is heading toward eternity.

SIMPLE SERMONS ON PROPHETIC THEMES; by W. Herschel Ford; Zondervan; 122 pp; $1.95.

These sermons are all centered around one theme—the return of our Lord and Savior. They were composed and preached over many years by Ford.

IN THESE LAST DAYS; by Kenneth S. Wuest; Eerdmans; 263 pp; $2.45. Wuest presents his own expanded translation of the text of II Peter, I,II,III John and Jude in the Greek New Testament. It is designed to help the student with no knowledge of the Greek to grasp a fuller meaning of the text.

PROPHETIC LIGHT IN THE PRESENT DARKNESS; by Kenneth S. Wuest; Eerdmans; 135 pp; $1.95. Wuest answers questions regarding the present world situation and what Biblical prophecy says about it. Written for Christian laymen everywhere who seek a knowledge of God and His Word for their lives.

APOCALYPTIC; by Leon Morris; Eerdmans; 87 pp; $1.95. Morris addresses himself to the characteristics of apocalyptic writings, the world from which they arose and their relation to the Gospel.

POPULATION, POLLUTION AND PROPHECY; by Leslie H. Woodson; Revell; 157 pp; $4.95. From his study of the contemporary problems of overpopulation and pollution, Woodson concludes that there is no human solution. There is a solution, however, and it can be found in prophetic Scriptures where God reveals His plan for man's eternal future.

JESUS IS COMING—GET READY CHRISTIAN!; by C.S. Lovett; Personal Christianity; 127 pp. This book alerts Christians to the fact that all must stand before the judgment seat of Christ and give an account of their works in the flesh. Lovett gives instructions for getting ready for that moment.

SECOND COMING; by Ralph Earle; Baker Book House; 88 pp; $.95. Dr. Earle has taken the major passages concerned with the Second Coming and given an exposition of each. The imminence of the Last Days is underscored but the author indulges in no speculative flights, naming of dates, or dogmatic assertions.

DAY X; by Kurt Koch; Kregel; 128 pp; $.95. Koch reviews the present world situation in the light of the nearness of the Lord's second coming.

EXPECT THESE THINGS; by Clyde W. Buxton; Revell; 151 pp; $2.95. What do prophetic Scriptures tell us about the eternal future of every Christian? This book attempts to unlock the truths of prophetic Scriptures and describes future events in terms understandable to the layman.

THE SECOND COMING BIBLE; by William E. Biederwolf; Baker Book House; 728 pp; $4.95. This book contains the complete text of every Scripture passage concerned with the second coming of Christ plus commentary on each verse.

FROM ETERNITY TO ETERNITY; by Erich Sauer; Eerdmans; 204 pp; $2.95. This book sets forth the historical unity of the Bible. Two further parts are added which deal with the question of the inspiration of the Bible and the millennium.

THE IMMINENT APPEARING OF CHRIST; by J. Barton Payne; Eerdmans; 191 pp; $3. The author assumes at all points the trustworthiness of Scripture, and is convinced that His coming will surely be accomplished in history.

GOD'S PROGRAM OF THE AGES: by Frederick A. Tatford; Kregel; 160 pp; $3.95. This is a readable handbook on the future, quoting and citing Scripture and clearly demonstrating the manner in which the entire Biblical picture fits together.

THE MARK OF THE BEAST; by Sydney Watson; Revell; 245 pp; $4.50. Although entirely fictional, the author has based his narrative on just what the Bible teaches concerning the Great Tribulation—that awful period of distress and woe that is coming upon this earth during the time when the Antichrist will rule with unhindered sway.

IN THE TWINKLING OF AN EYE; by Sydney Watson; Revell; 250 pp; $4.50. Here is an imaginative and dramatic, yet true-to-Scripture account of what will transpire on this earth at the coming of the Lord.

PROPHETIC TRUTH UNFOLDING TODAY; Charles L. Feinberg, editor; Revell; 160 pp; $4.50. This book contains a message of hope for all who put their faith and trust in Jesus Christ and look to His return with eager longing. These messages were presented at the Fifth Congress on Prophecy and addressed to Christians of this day and hour.

THE APOCALYPSE; by E.W. Bullinger; Revell; 741 pp; $7.95. A non-traditional exposition of the Apocalypse based on the foundation that John saw the events as they will take place in "the Day of the Lord." Bullinger writes on the assumption that in order to get a true understanding of any passage, or book, the interpretation of the words must be determined by the scope of the context.

THE RETURN OF CHRIST; by G.C. Berkouwer; Eerdmans; 453 pp; $9.95. The author addresses himself to a wide range of questions Christians ask about end times, and speaks to issues much in evidence today.

ENCYCLOPEDIA OF BIBLICAL PROPHECY; by J. Barton Payne; Harper and Row; 754 pp; $19.95. Payne discusses every verse of prophetic matter in Scripture, and features a complete list of all the scriptural prophecies pertaining to Christ.

THE THEOCRATIC KINGDOM (3 volumes); by George N.H. Peters; Kregel; 2175 pp; $39.95. A work on predictive prophecy in which statements are heavily supported with relevant references. Over 4,000 authors are quoted in these volumes which treat the subject with depth, clearness and understanding.

A COMPANION TO THE NEW SCOFIELD REFERENCE BIBLE; by E. Schuyler English; Oxford University Press; 165 pp; $4.50. In his examination of the Bible, Dr. English moves from the account in Genesis of the origin of the universe and the creation of man, to the Revelation. His purpose is to enable the reader to harmonize all parts of the Bible, to fit each into its proper place and to understand some of the obscure passages.

BOOKLETS

THE BEAST; Chick Publications; 47 pp; $.15 ea. A small booklet which illustrates and tells, with references, what will happen at the rapture and during the tribulation.

OUTLINE STUDIES ON THE RAPTURE; by Ed Sanders; Biblical Research Institute; 31 pp; $1. A series of studies designed to examine crucial questions and topics associated with the Lord's Return. The pretribulational rapture theory is examined and a Scriptural alternative is given.

THE BIBLICAL BASIS FOR THE POSTTRIBULATION RAPTURE; by Del Birkey; Biblical Research Institute; 17 pp; $1. A study guide on the posttribulation view.

A SIMPLE PICTURE OF THE FUTURE; by William W. Orr; Scripture Press; 32 pp; $.39. A brief survey on prophecy with references listed.

THE BLESSED HOPE; by William C. Thomas; Biblical Research Institute; 47 pp. Three messages designed to present the Lord's return as the Blessed Hope of the Christian church.

A SIGN OF CHRIST'S IMPENDING ADVENT; by Herbert W. Butt; Biblical Research Institute; 27 pp. The author reminds us that we are in this world to demonstrate the reality of our saving union with Christ, and to look forward to Christ's return.

CHARTS

BIBLE DIGEST CHARTS; by Charles W. Slemming; Kregel; 139 pp; $5.95. Sixty-two Bible charts presenting a pictorial outline of each book of the Bible is divided into what is known as Biblical Analysis and Biblical Synthesis: the art of breaking down and the art of putting together, respectively.

THE EXPANDED PANORAMA BIBLE STUDY COURSE; by Alfred Thompson Eade; Revell; 192 pp; $5.95. This book is designed to help the reader better visualize the continuity and significance of Bible events. Introducing each unit is a chart pictorially summarizing the material treated.

THE NEW "PANORAMA" BIBLE STUDY

SERIES (set of four); by Alfred Thompson Eade; Revell. 1) *A STUDY OF DISPENSATIONAL TRUTH;* An illustrated guide presenting the key passage of Scripture, arranged in chronological order, unfolding the story of God's revealed will and purpose of the ages. 2) *THE STUDY OF ANGELOLOGY;* Charts combine with text in this survey of Scriptural revelation to depict the activity of the Angelic Hosts and the attendant doctrine of "Demonology." 3) *THE SECOND COMING OF CHRIST;* This study course on eschatology contains an array of predictions and prophecies. The unfolding of Bible revelation and the greatness and glory of God are presented in chart and text. 4) *THE BOOK OF REVELATION;* A visual interpretation of the Apocalypse with illustrations and charts reflecting the Divine events as prophesied in Scripture, together with inspired commentary and concise text.

THE PROPHECY MAP OF WORLD HISTORY; by J. Barton Payne; Harper and Row; $2.95. The 737 subjects of Biblical prophecy are represented according to the order of their fulfillment in history, whether past, present or future.

CASSETTES ALSO PREPARE YOU FOR CHRIST'S SECOND COMING

Along with the books, films and records concerned with prophecy, publishers also are concentrating on cassette tapes. Dramatic narratives, in-depth studies and scriptural explanations are some features in the tapes listed below.

Bethany Fellowship

THE VISION; by Dave Wilkerson; $3.95 each. Wilkerson tells what to expect in this end time generation.

PROPHECY, THE CATALYST OF REVIVAL; by Arthur Bloomfield; $3.95 each. A message indicating that the actual fulfillment of prophecy, acting as a catalyst, will speed up revival and the spreading of the Gospel.

THE NEXT GREAT EVENT; by Kathryn Kuhlman; $3.95 each. Fulfilled prophecy is proof of the authenticity of God's Word—and Kathryn Kuhlman shows from the prophetic Word that we are in the most exciting days of history, immediately preceding the return of Jesus.

THIS IS THE RAPTURE GENERATION; by Hilton Sutton; $3.95 each. Without setting dates, the speaker presents startling fulfillments of Bible prophecy which indicate that our generation is the rapture generation.

YOU CAN UNDERSTAND REVELATION; by Hilton Sutton; $3.95. The speaker gives a number of simple keys which will help you to discover the message of the book of Revelation. There is strong emphasis on teaching about the second coming of Jesus, the tribulation, the Antichrist, the battle of Armageddon, the millennium, and the new heaven and earth.

Maranatha Tape Library

COMING WAR WITH RUSSIA; Ezekiel 38; $2.75 each.

SIGNS OF HIS COMING; Psalm 102:16, $2.75 each.

HE SHALL REIGN; Revelation 11:15; $2.75 each.

One Way Library

THE LATE GREAT PLANET EARTH; by Hal Lindsey; Set of 6 tapes for $19.95. Lindsey discusses the amazing developments which are taking place in Europe and Asia, and the remarkable discoveries of his most recent tour of the Middle East.

THE HOLY SPIRIT IN THE LAST DAYS; by Hal Lindsey; set of 6 tapes for $19.95. An in-depth study of a most controversial subject—the nature and work of the Holy Spirit—which will be of "tremendous value to the individual who seeks a closer walk with the Lord in these last days."

SATAN IS ALIVE AND WELL ON PLANET EARTH; by Hal Lindsey; Set of 6, $19.95. Lindsey delivers a lively set of cassette material with an in-depth Biblical study of Satan, his origin, methods and destiny.

Derek Prince Publications

CLIMAX IN FOUR PHASES; by Derek Prince; 86 minutes; $3.95 each. Four successive phases are discussed: repentance, refreshing, restoration and return of Christ, also the parallel between the first and second coming of Christ and Isaiah's picture of a glorious church coming forth at the close of the age.

DIVINE DESTINY FOR THIS NATION (U.S.A.) AND THIS GENERATION; by Derek Prince; 58 minutes; $3.95. Each nation and each generation needs a direct revelation of God's special purposes for them. At this time a special generation is emerging, foretold in Scripture.

PROPHECY: GOD'S TIME-MAP; by Derek Prince; 59 minutes; $3.95. Prince parallels the restoration of Israel and the Church since 1900.

Triumphant Records—One Way Ministries

THE RAPTURE; by Jack W. Hester. Recorded "on the spot" in what could well be your city, is this narrative drama of a most astonishing moment to come in history.

Word

THE COSMIC DRAMA; Studies in Revelation; by Herschel H. Hobbs; four cassettes and response manual; $24.95. Explains difficult symbols and clarifies historical illusions by looking at Revelation through the eyes of the first century Christians.

NEW PERSON, NEW CHURCH, NEW WORLD; by Martin E. Marty; four cassettes and response manual; $24.95. Depicts what is happening to alter peoples' way of looking at the world.